The Truth Zone:

Stories of

Adventure and Misadventure

Climbing

California's Highest Peaks

Adrian Crane and Deborah E. Steinberg

******

ISBN: 978-0-578-75578-6

DEDICATION

To all who wander.

The Truth Zone

CONTENTS

Foreword...i

Introduction v

Mt Shasta In Winter...1

Mt Sill...11

Middle Palisade..19

Mt Whitney and Mt Muir...27

Langley in Winter..35

North Palisade and Polemonium Peak 43

Split Mountain In Winter..53

Williamson and Tyndall 63

Thunderbolt and Starlight...73

Williamson...87

Russell and Split..97

White Mountain in Winter...107

White Mountain in Summer...115

Postscript...121

Acknowledgments 125

Timeline 127

Peaks ranked by Difficulty 129

Peaks ranked by Height 130

Blister Prevention 131

Food Planning for Mountaineering 135

Gear Checklist 139

About The Authors 141

The Truth Zone

FOREWORD
Steve Porcella
Co-author of Climbing California's 14,000' peaks.

Why climb a mountain? Or, why climb one or all of California's 14,000' peaks? The most quoted response regarding 'why mountain climb?', was made by George Mallory, in responding to the question of, "why try to climb Everest?" - a mountain he would perish on a year later, George replied, "Because it's there." For these peaks in California, and the question of why climb them, one obvious reason is that they are the 15 highest mountains in the great state of California. But a rational person would respond that climbing is a lot of work, with risk and some luck involved, and while the view from the summit may be spectacular it also can be hidden by clouds. So, back to the question, why climb one, or all 15 of these peaks? In truth, the answer is as varied and different as we are. Some reasons are deep and complex, and some are as simple as George Mallory's, "Because it's there." And, to make things more complicated, the reason why you climbed your first 14er may change when you are going for your 5th, or your 15th. And, when you are asked later in life, why did you climb them all, your response may be completely different from that moment that you crested your first 14er summit.

Starting in the spring of 1989 and well into 1991, Cameron Burns and I started work on the first, historical climbing guidebook on California's 14,000' peaks. Not much was known about these mountains back then, people did not even know how many there were. Each is unique, different, and worthy of a bid for its summit. Cameron and I threw ourselves at these mountains, circumnavigating all and climbing sixty-five different routes, twelve of which were new routes - in total, we climbed about a third of all the known routes. Sierra chroniclers have called our breakneck pursuit "The Blitz," and I won't lie, it was; we simply could not get enough of them, and it wasn't until we were out of money and exhausted that we walked away, our arms full of stories, experiences and memories. It remains to this day my fondest climbing memory. Please know, gentle reader, that these mountains are everyone's mountains, and the stories you create on them are your stories and that you have a right to share and tell your stories to others, just as the authors do here in this book. These mountains have so much to give to the human race, and it is all of our responsibility to take care of them, speak up for them and to help keep them in their native state for future generations.

As you hold this book, contemplating purchasing it, you may know ahead of time that you want to climb these peaks and perhaps you are looking for additional information. Alternatively, you may have no desire to climb these mountains, but you want to know what it is like to have that goal and what it takes to safely accomplish these summits. This book provides answers to both of these possible scenarios. This book will help you understand how a group of people, with different skills, experience, and perceptions can come together to safely climb up them, and down them.

This book is written in a running commentary, so that you feel you are there suffering or enjoying the environment or the company of others. In an adventurous style, they climb these peaks in different seasons and conditions, taking on the different challenges while working together. Most times they succeed in their summit bids, and sometimes they turn back to climb another day. Both situations are important to study, for future summiteers. The authors choose easy routes and hard routes, pushing their skill and confidence levels. This is notable because many believe climbing is not about the summit, but rather the journey and experience of chasing that goal. Some of the best moments are when they push the envelope with weather and conditions, only to fall well short of their goal. These are humbling moments, but in the end, the authors and their team members discover greater awareness and a new respect of the high Sierra, including, a greater appreciation of their future accomplishment.

If you look for more in life than a job, a career, or material things; if you look for insight, enlightenment, and if you have questions that may or may not have answers, then this book is for you. For in the pages of this book, you will find folks that climbed these peaks for many different reasons. They share their experiences, which includes a lesser known reason for climbing mountains - that of climbing for others who had or still have their own burden to carry, in this case, a burden of cancer, a burden that involves a mountain not made of rock and ice.

When George Mallory had more time to muse, he was able to elaborate on the contradiction that is inherent in climbing. He wrote, "...nothing will come of it. We shall not bring back a single bit of gold or silver, not a gem... [but], we do not live to eat and make money, we eat and make money to live." [We do it] "...for the spirit of adventure, to keep alive the soul of man." I think about this frequently in my own way, this concept of 'climbing, to keep alive the souls of humans.' It's too easy and simplistic to think of climbing as a selfish sport, and it is wrong to think of it that way. I used to take young college graduates, destined for graduate or medical schools, out climbing, and while walking past big granite walls, I would point above and describe that I climbed them. To the stunned look on their faces, I always replied, "because I accomplished that, you can do anything that you think you can." The physics of climbing, that which involves the physical exertion against the rarified air, the exposure to danger, the management of safety, all contribute to a heightened awareness and sense of self. Many mountain climbers describe these moments and feelings as exhilaration, and a sense of successful management of doubt and fear, which is a unique feeling that lasts forever. The authors of this book, describe climbing for those that suffered from cancer and through their climb, and their toils, they describe a shared sense of community, a connection and a type of support for those that fought the bravest of battles against a disease that is relentless, merciless, and that takes far too many people before their time.

Keep your soul and the souls of others alive, and climb. Climb one or all of the 14,000 peaks of California both for yourself, your partner, and for those that cannot. Be the person that says to others, "you can do anything that you think you can, and I am an example of that truth." Use this book as a guide to accomplishing one or all of these summits. Follow the 'accepting and inclusive' camaraderie of this book, foster your own shared experiences, be open to the differences in others, and think about a unique reason that you want to climb these peaks. Climbing for others is noble and selfless. The human experience is unlimited, and sharing summits with those that are present or not present is one of the most fulfilling things we can do in this world, and, it feeds the soul.

Steve Porcella
Co-author of *Climbing California's 14,000' peaks.*

The Truth Zone

INTRODUCTION

Stepping outside the tent, Deborah was surprised to find herself engulfed by perfect quiet; the midnight air was buoyed by silvery light silently pouring from a full moon. Awakening to this calm was unexpected, as Mt. Shasta is usually tossed by wintry winds. The steep, icy slopes which she and the group had ascended less than 24 hours prior, glowed dimly with a fluorescent blue hue, precipitously plunging towards the lights of Shasta City. In the distance, she could just identify the silhouette of Mt. Lassen. Despite the moonlight, the stars burned stubbornly above, exposed by the absence of cloud cover. The illumination was like that between two worlds, that of sunshine, and that of night. She felt like an animal with night vision, able to observe potential prey and predators. The silence was punctuated only by her boots crunching through the crystallized snow and the shuffle of a marmot dashing away with a scrap of food discovered near the camp stove. Deborah became aware of the chill and yanked her hat further down over her ears, lifted her hood, and buried her perpetually cold hands deep into her pockets. She realized she wasn't as exhausted as she should have been, having climbed 9 hours and 3,700 vertical feet to reach the summit before returning to camp; rather, she was buzzing with a sense of accomplishment.

The summit earlier that day had almost been a failure.

The group of four was roped together, marching en masse towards the summit, their pace determined by the slowest individual. One person in the climbing party had difficulty moving at a pace that would reach the summit by 1:00 pm., the cutoff time for a safe return. Then the straps on Deborah's crampons kept loosening and falling off. Every few minutes she had to stop to readjust or put them back on, slowing down the group even more.

Crampons are crucial gear: spiked metal boot fixtures critical to securing one's step across hardened snow and ice.

Despite the hindered pace, the group pushed on towards the summit. Trudging upwards, they came upon another party of three who had the same challenge with mismatched speeds. The groups roped their two slowest climbers together so everyone could move safely at their own pace.

Finally, one of Deborah's crampons broke entirely. She was disappointed that she would have to give up, abandon the group, and turn back having come all that way! Not only that, the journey uphill was so treacherous that to even consider descending with only one crampon was frightening.

Deborah then remembered that her climbing partner Adrian always carried a bit of string and duct tape. On the brink of defeat, she sat on a boulder protruding from the ice as he attempted to salvage her crampon. Miraculously, he was successful, and Deborah felt a renewed sense of hope. It was then she pointed to a ridge looming 500 vertical feet above the group and told Adrian, "I think I can make it." She stood up, and the group carried on.

The small group of frozen weary mountaineers, verging on success, painstakingly ascended the final steep crag. Victoriously, one by one, they perched in the thin air on the ice-rimmed rocks of the summit and swapped congratulations. Shortly after snapping a few photos, their concentration, which had been fixated on the rocky zenith, shifted towards the downward trek and getting home safely.

Awash in such mental sunshine, as Deborah descended she asked "So, Adrian, what's our next adventure?" Thus was born the bold and conjectural plan to summit all fifteen of the California Fourteeners.

Reflecting on the day's accomplishment in the stillness of midnight, Deborah thought to herself that the success was really all about determination with a little luck thrown in. Over the next few years, she would discover how much determination and luck she would need to attain such a tremendous goal.......

There are times when the accomplishment of one small goal leads to a completely unexpected journey, and that is the case here. Summiting Mt. Shasta in the winter of 2008 inspired the challenge of climbing all the peaks with a summit above 14,000 feet in California. In all of the contiguous United States, there are only three states with mountains over 14,000 feet. Colorado is dotted with 54 of them, California boasts 15, and Washington State claims Mt. Rainier. The tallest of these is California's Mt.Whitney, grazing the sky at 14,494 feet. Each mountain presents its own unique set of challenges, not limited to altitude and endurance. This is the story of Deborah Steinberg and Adrian Crane and their four-year-long journey of overcoming these challenges as they climbed California's fifteen 'fourteeners' in pursuit of adventure, wilderness and a cure for cancer.

By the time he relocated to Modesto, California, Adrian "Ados" Crane was a seasoned adventurer and had been mountaineering and peak-bagging for many years. He always entertained the idea of climbing all the 14,000-foot mountains in the Golden State, having climbed all of Colorado's Fourteeners in 1993. While idly checking out mountaineering books he had come across a picture of the pinnacle of Starlight Peak, and plans for how to scale that treacherous summit block frequently filled his daydreams. Time passed and concrete plans to attack the mountains never materialized. Occasional climbs of the well-known fourteeners, Mt. Shasta and Mt. Whitney occurred, but Adrian was side-tracked with other outdoor adventures.

The backdrop of this pursuit is Modesto, California; a sprawling suburb, positioned almost exactly in the center of the State. Within its small-town feel and flat, wide, leafy streets are to be found a loose-knit group of runners, adventure racers, hikers, climbers, and outdoorsy people. When the time comes to head to the mountains, there is a good group of reliable people to be found in Modesto and the surrounding areas. These individuals, many who repeatedly joined in on the summit attempts described in this book, have proved invaluable in their encouragement, support and companionship on this quest.

Deborah Steinberg lives in Modesto and enjoyed light outdoor adventures like backpacking and camping. She crossed paths with Adrian many times through the town's Adventure Club. Over the years, Deborah would occasionally organize a snow camping trip or backpack weekend with family and friends and mention, around a campfire, that she still wanted to climb Mount Shasta.

A lot of people ask how Deborah got into mountaineering in the first place, because truthfully it is not as common as you would think to find women climbing technical mountains. She likes to joke, "I fell in with the wrong crowd." In 1990, Deborah and her husband Ross (who was then her boyfriend) moved to Modesto, CA. Yes, Modesto is in California, a state with a very hip reputation, but Modesto is anything but hip. Unlike its cooler city cousins Los Angeles and San Francisco, Modesto, being in the center of the state is most definitely the "country cousin". Located at the heart of the great Central Valley where much of the country's food is grown, people are friendly and laid back, but decidedly not "cool." It is a place where neighbors knock on your door to deliver a bag of plums or tomatoes because their backyard garden is overflowing. Pretty much everyone in Modesto has a small garden in their backyard, or at least a few fruit trees. Like most of the Central Valley, the soil is fertile, and home to almonds, walnuts, corn, tomatoes, and dairy cattle. Modesto is not a place you would expect to encounter mountaineers. The economy relies on farmers, teachers, merchants, and Gallo wine. Most of its residents head west to the big City of San Francisco when they look for a weekend away.

However, just east of Modesto, the Sierra Nevada Mountains tower above the state in a 300-mile range, running from north to south. On a clear day in Modesto, you can see the mountains low on the horizon, but not many residents pay them much attention. One famous Modesto resident who did was the late Royal Robbins, a revered pioneer in big wall rock climbing in Yosemite. But, for this town, a critical mass on the rock climbing connection was never quite attained. Instead, Modesto celebrates vintage cars, the Americana tradition of cruising, and "American Graffiti," created by Modesto-born George Lucas. It also retains a dubious distinction based on several heinous crimes and a particularly high rate of car thefts.

The secret advantage of living in Modesto is that if you do manage to have a decent job, the cost of living is so much more reasonable than in the Bay Area or Southern California that you can live quite comfortably and without the long commutes of a more urban lifestyle. You find your friends are all practically neighbors, making meeting up for lunch or dinner uncomplicated and laying a solid foundation for clubs and social groups. Shortly after moving to Modesto, Ross and Deb heard about the newly established Adventure Club, founded by Adrian Crane and Joann Grether. The premise of the Adventure Club was to bring together people who loved the outdoors and were not afraid to get a little cold, wet, and dirty. She joined at the club's second meeting, and quickly volunteered to create the monthly newsletters.

Before Deborah had even met him, she had heard about Adrian; that he had participated in all the famed Eco-Challenge expedition adventure races, set a record for speed-climbing the Colorado 14ers, and that he and his brother had run across the entire Himalayas and written a book about it. She had also heard he had climbed Mt. Shasta. At the time that she met him, Adrian's polite British accent, thick red hair, rather large glasses, and a handlebar mustache made him a doppelganger to Sir Nigel Archibald Thornberry from the Nickelodeon animated series The Wild Thornberrys. Her first real bonafide adventure with the group was a snow camping trip on Mt. Shasta in 1990. With a goal of reaching Helen Lake to camp, they snowshoed out of Bunny Flat, but made it just above Horse Camp where they set up tents for the night. Around 3:00 am, the group could hear Adrian and Jeff scuffling around in the snow as they set off for the summit, while the rest promptly rolled over and fell back to sleep. The next morning Deb and her husband realized their contact lenses had frozen in their cases overnight, giving them an excuse to shove them down their sleeping bags and sleep in for another 10 minutes. Ross and Deb relaxed for the rest of the day, exploring on snowshoes and reading in the tent. Just before sunset, Adrian and Jeff returned from a successful climb of the mountain, and the group quickly fired up the stoves to make them a hot drink. About ten years later, Adrian asked Ross and Deb if they would like to climb Mt. Shasta during the summer via Avalanche Gulch. Well, Ross loves the wilderness, but hates to suffer, so, as he thought about a 3:00 am departure by headlamp in the freezing cold, he politely declined. Deb, however, always willing to latch onto other's well-made plans, jumped at the chance. The climb was unlike anything she had ever done before. She did indeed awaken at 3:00 am to rope up her harness, strap on her crampons, and head out into the dark, climbing an incredibly steep icy slope for what felt like hours. What she did not realize was that this was truly just the beginning of her journey in so many ways. Giddy and dizzy from the thin air, after what felt like an eternity of slogging up steep hills, she stood on the summit of Mt. Shasta and gazed at the incredible view of Shastina and the coast range far off in the distance.

Wham! Deborah had summit fever, and by the time she had descended the mountain and was eating burgers at a local diner, she was already planning with the group to attempt a climb of Mt. Shasta in winter.

You would think that Adrian would be a bit snobby, with the mass of adventurous feats he has accomplished in the areas of running, mountaineering, and adventure racing, and would want to hang out with only accomplished athletes. On the contrary, he can be pretty willing to, quite literally, "show the ropes" to capable newcomers, of which Deborah can attest. He can be exceptionally polite and patient, which must be required traits for all British nationals. Once, with the help of the famed Yosemite big wall climber Royal Robbins, he hosted a tree-climbing clinic at his house for Deborah's Girl Scout troop of 12 year-olds. After setting up the ropes with Royal, Adrian snuck into the house and came out with a tray of cucumber sandwiches, all crust-less and pointed. He is extremely sociable, likes to make clever puns in his British accent, and is always good for a story when the rest of us are a bit miserable slogging through scree or up an icefield. We would hear, "I'm so pleased the weather has been so lovely for us," "I was so chuffed when we made it to the top of that icy ridge," or, "Give me a moment, I have to go to the loo." He loves to chat about current events and politics, and philosophize about solutions to various social dilemmas. Above all, Adrian likes to challenge his body and gear so that he is reasonably comfortable even when the outside conditions are extremely poor. If the going is too easy, he secretly hopes for a "bit of weather" to stir things up a little so he can test out a new shelter or wind jacket. Adrian is all about going lightweight. If he thought he could save a little weight by cutting out the labels of his jacket, he would do so. More than once he has shown up for a backpacking trip without a sleeping bag, covering himself with backpack, jackets, and all his clothing, in an effort to see if he could manage the night comfortably in the 40-degree chilly air without having to beg to get into anyone's already crowded tent. He has spent many a winter weekend climbing Mt. Shasta in conditions so bad that no one else would dare to go up there with him, all so that he could "tune-up" for his next adventure on Aconcagua or Mt. Everest. This also explains why, when climbing the 14ers, our group did not usually take the easiest route unless we had already failed along a more difficult way, and that we climbed the California 14ers in winter and spring conditions too, not solely during the favorable conditions of summer.

What allowed us to venture off into the vast wilderness seeking the highest summit was excellent navigational skills on the part of Adrian and others who climbed with us as well, such as Ray and Mark. We used a map and compass only, not because GPS wasn't available to us, but because it added to the challenge, the batteries don't run out, and was more in the style of an adventure race. It turns out that mountaineering is excellent training for numerous athletic endeavors, and many an adventure racing friend would join our expeditions. Regardless of whether you use a map or GPS, in mountaineering it is not always obvious which route will lead you up the mountain safely. Sometimes picking the correct chute will make the difference between a summit or not, since there could be an unexpected cliff or insurmountable wall of rock that would prevent progress. We all had regular day-jobs, so staying an extra few days to go back by a different route was not usually an option. Sometimes there were failures, and it would take more than one trip up the mountain before we tackled the summit, but this only made success all the sweeter.

Since 2001, Deb had been the leader of her older daughter's Girl Scout troop, and they had a reputation for going on the most adventurous outings; rock climbing, kayaking, and snowshoeing. Deb's friend Kelly Gregerson from Girl Scouts, who knew early on about Deborah's quest to climb all of the California 14ers, gave her Barbara Washburn's memoir *The Accidental Adventurer*. Barbara describes the story of how she became the first woman to climb Mt. McKinley and several other mountains in Alaska as the wife of famed mountaineer Bradford Washburn. Barbara was not in a leadership position on any of these climbs but was still a respected and integral member of the climbing team. Deborah felt a connection to Barbara who noted that, as the least experienced member of the team, she just needed more perseverance. Another friend from Girl Scouts was Kristen Machado, who Deb would occasionally join on early morning runs with a group of friends. Kristen was an extremely upbeat, kind, and responsible person with a heartwarming smile, exactly who you want for your daughter's Girl Scout leader. She was also not afraid to be forthright, which was admired. One morning, Kristen was not there. She had undergone surgery for a cancerous tumor in her arm, and Deborah did not realize at the time what a serious battle this was to be for her.

When plans were casually announced to climb the rest of the California 14ers, not surprisingly, most of our group of regular adventurers were "in" for at least part of it. With Deborah's friend Kristen in mind, Deborah and Adrian discussed the positive aspects of dedicating the climbs to those whose lives were touched by cancer in hopes of raising awareness and funds for cancer research at STOP CANCER. Thus "Climb for a Cure" was born. Not only was there a goal of climbing the rest of the 14ers, there was now a purpose and a vision to keep them motivated.

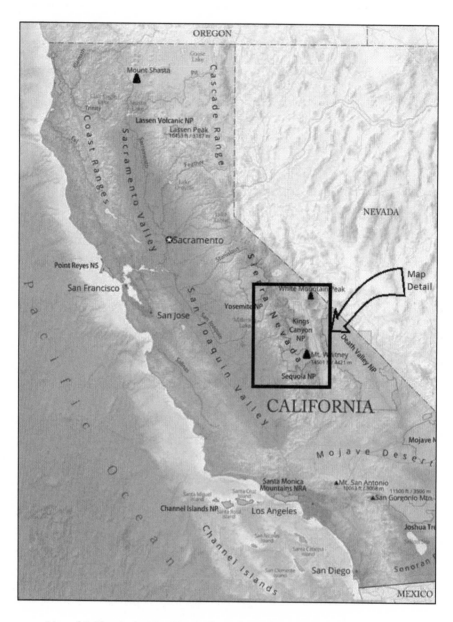

Map of California showing Mount Shasta, Mt Whitney and White Mountain,
The remaining peaks are shown in the map detail.

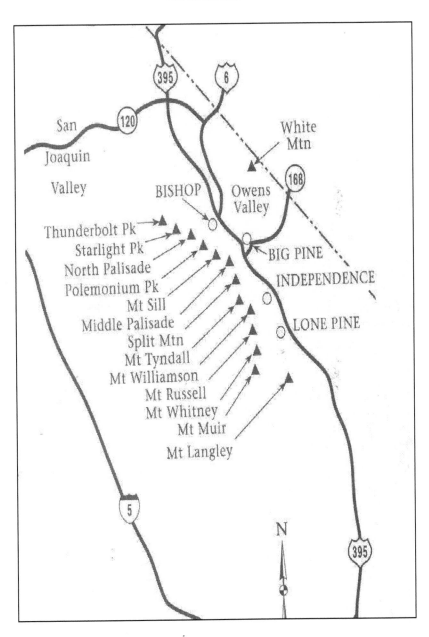

Map detail showing 14 of the 15 California 14ers, Mount Shasta is not shown.

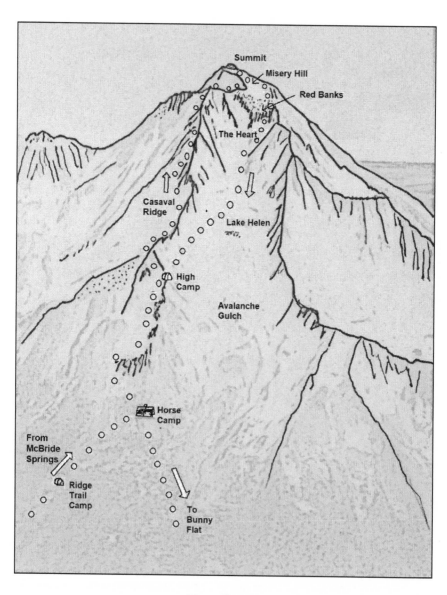

Mount Shasta.

Chapter 1
MT SHASTA IN WINTER

14,180 feet
February 15th-18th, 2008
Summary: Successful Shasta winter trip with great weather on the Casaval Ridge Route.
This was the seminal adventure that would spawn Climb for a Cure and the quest to climb
the rest of the California peaks over 14,000 feet.
Our Team: Adrian Crane, Deborah Steinberg, Derek Castle, Carey Gregg, Brien
Crothers, Ray Kablanow, Vance Roget, and Mark Richardson, Christopher Crane,
Johnathan Crane, Melissa Griffith, Andrew "Griff" Griffith, and Brian B, "the
hitchhiker".

Our first attempt at climbing Mt. Shasta in winter was the previous February of 2007 but unfortunately it was not meant to be that year. Both Derek and Carey were suffering from altitude sickness, and we got off to a late start, losing steam and turning back at about 1500 vertical feet from the summit. Deborah decided that if she was to summit in winter on the more difficult Casaval Ridge Route, she was going to have to prepare and get in shape. Many of the others were long distance runners or adventure racers. Deborah joined a gym and spent hours a week on the stairmaster for months, and faithfully worked on leg presses and leg extensions. During her trail running she focused on hills and endurance. For the 2008 trip, we planned to allow four days in order to have an extra day to acclimatize and make the trip easier on summit day. This turned out to be a lucky decision since the road to the Bunny Flat trailhead parking lot was closed. They hadn't cleared the road of snow yet, so we had to start out lower at McBride Springs. Our intended destination the first night was Horse Camp, but, being forced to climb in from the lower area, we had to gain an additional 3000 feet and several miles to get to it compared to the hike in from Bunny Flat. It was 1:30 in the afternoon before we headed out from McBride Springs, having left Modesto at 6:00 am. We were blessed with fantastic clear and calm weather which lasted the entire weekend, almost unheard of on Shasta in February or

Deborah on Casaval Ridge, Mount Shasta

any other time of year. We set out with sleds so we could pull more gear and planned to set up a storage tent at a lower camp. The group at that point was comprised of Deborah, Adrian, Derek, Carey, Mark, Ray, Vance and Brien Crothers. Vance is a physical rehabilitation and sports medicine physician, but also an accomplished marathoner and ultra-runner. He was our chief sled dog, and Carey, assisting with the sled, had a hard time keeping up with his brisk pace. On the first evening we were only able to climb until dark, so at 5:30 pm we found ourselves setting up camp on a narrow ridge in the trees about 500 vertical feet below Horse Camp.

Later that night, Andrew and Melissa Griffiths joined us after trekking to our camp in the dark. Adrian was still waiting on his sons Johnathan and Christopher to arrive and catch up and was texting them in the middle of the night because he still had phone service. Adrian, Derek, and Deborah shared a tent, and were joking quite a bit the first night. Sometimes we would hear people laughing at our jokes from other tents, so our spirits were pretty high. That night, the raccoons raided our stash of food, and animal theft ended up plaguing us the rest of the trip. We awoke the next morning in a leisurely fashion and, donning snow shoes, set out for our advanced base camp at 9500 feet. We had seen the camp last year occupied by a climbing school and thought it would be the highest camp that would be possible before summit day. We passed Horse Camp after about an hour and picked up a "hitchhiker" climber there, Brian B., who had been waiting for friends to join him. They had not shown but as he was still keen to try for the summit, we welcomed him onto our team. As well, Jonathan and Christopher finally caught up to us. Unfortunately, Jonathan was sick even before he left the trailhead, so he was not feeling well when he arrived at camp. It was steep in some sections on the way to the next camp, and we were all a little exhausted after climbing about four hours that day. As we climbed and the snow got harder, we switched our snowshoes for crampons and cached our snowshoes at last year's campsite so we would not have to carry their weight all the way to our advanced base camp. All 13 of us camped on a saddle that had gorgeous views in every direction; to the town of Shasta below, the mountain itself above, and all around, the mountains beyond. As we discussed strategy for summiting the following day, Derek and Ray felt that they were not strong enough to try for the summit, and, since Jonathan was sick, Christopher decided to go back with his brother the next day as well. On the way up to camp, we noticed distant ant-like beings near the parking lot signaling that the road to Bunny Flat had been opened that day. Ray and Derek decided that they would descend on Sunday, taking the tent that Adrian, Derek, and Deborah had slept in, then travel down to our original camp. There they would pick up the storage tent and sleds and move the vehicles up to Bunny Flat so that when we descended after Summit Day we would not have to travel as far. The rest of us broke up into climbing parties of three: Adrian, Carey, and Deborah; Melissa, Andrew, and Brian B.; Vance, Mark, & Brien. Deborah noticed that with the altitude she had lost all of her usually robust appetite, but it was just as well since she also noticed that she had left her food at the lower camp! From Saturday night on Deborah relied on others' generous donations of food. Fortunately for her, Mark had brought a huge surplus of food, and was more than willing to share so he wouldn't be stuck with carrying the weight down the mountain.

Johnathan Crane on the slopes of Mount Shasta

After going to bed full from all the leftover food handouts, Deborah awoke with the group at 3:00 am, and was very anxious. Her legs felt like Jell-O and she was worried she was getting a cold. She forced herself to choke down a breakfast cookie, knowing as soon as we started exerting any energy she would need it. At 4:30 am, we strapped on our crampons. Soon after we began climbing with headlamps, Deborah started experiencing trouble keeping the crampons on her boots. She had to regularly check them and tighten them and Adrian was constantly helping to re-strap them. Our parties were roped up together for safety since most of our climbing was on the treacherously icy north side of Casaval ridge. Deborah consciously decided not to look down as she followed with Adrian in front and Carey behind.

After a few hours, Carey started to fatigue. Being in the middle, there were times when Adrian was pulling on Deb and she was dragging Carey. Finally, we caught up with Vance, Mark, and Brien C., who were in a similar situation in that Brien was starting to fall back while Vance and Mark wanted to go full-steam ahead. At first, Adrian suggested that Deb rope up with Vance and Mark and Adrian go on with Brian and Carey, but she vigorously protested. Vance is older than Deborah and has been in a few bad accidents where he has actually had to recover in a hospital, but you wouldn't know it by seeing him that day. Vance trains for all sorts of endurance races by dragging a truck tire and was unstoppable on this particular trip. Only Mark was able to keep up with him since he was training for expedition-length multi-day adventure races. "Nope, nope, and nope," she thought. "There was no way I could keep up with those two as sled dogs." Deborah suggested we rope up Carey with Brien and create a new party, but Adrian had not brought another rope. Finally, Adrian got the idea to cut one of our ropes. Thus, we set off as three parties of two persons that were better matched for speed.

We were now at 12,500 feet elevation, and Deborah had an epiphany. She was exhausted, but we had climbed nearly 3500 vertical feet of the 5100 we would need to climb. She realized that 1600 more vertical feet must be doable, until Adrian mentioned that it would be about 3 hours longer. But, she thought about how all these circumstances of perfect weather, being in great shape, and not being sick made it a "now or never" situation. If she couldn't summit this weekend, she never would. So, although it may have been the altitude talking, Deborah promised Adrian that he never had to take her to any summit again if he got her there this weekend. As a matter of fact, she promised him she would never even bother to attempt another mountain again! Soon after, her crampons actually broke, and Deborah thought she would have to face up to not seeing her dream through. Fortunately, Adrian was able to rig up a workable repair with a little string, and we continued on. Deborah laughed when it dawned on her that every gear list Adrian had ever sent out for any adventure included "string" and she had never before known why. However, now she was convinced Adrian could write a book on "How to Fix Anything with String and Duct Tape." Deborah was roused from her thoughts as she noticed we faced a horrifically steep slope ahead of us. Deb told Adrian, "The top of that ridge is my first goal." Once we reached the top of the first goal, she felt a huge sense of accomplishment and determination.

It was extremely windy at the top of that ridge, but we moved down a few feet to a much more sheltered area. We had met up with Andrew, Melissa, and Brian B. who had been moving along nicely at this point, although Andrew was now starting to feel the effects of elevation as we were well over 13,000 feet. We snacked a bit as we sized up the aptly-named "Misery Hill" that consists of icy loose shell-like scree that sounds like china breaking as it rolls down the hill behind each step. To get there we first had to climb downhill about 300 feet, which felt like such a waste of elevation and energy. Deborah saw others ahead of us traversing the steep icy hill, and asked, "Should I traverse it in switchbacks?" Adrian said that no, you might as well just go straight up.

"Straight up? Really? Do I have to go to the top of the hill, or can we just go around it?" "All the way to the top" was his response. Deb ate some more high-energy foods and started out ahead of Adrian, slogging along 5 steps at a time, then resting for a few moments before continuing. We discovered that "Misery Hill" is aptly named, and continued at a slow but consistent pace. Eventually, Deb looked back to find most of the group quite a ways behind, to her surprise. Finally, at the top of Misery Hill, the summit came into view. We really only had to traverse a spooky ice-strewn plain the size of 3 football fields and then climb a little 200-foot rock that was the summit. It seemed to take an eternity to traverse the ice field, which had the consistency of soft sand.

We passed a few eerie fumarole vents which greeted us with warm steam. This felt ironic to Deborah, since here we were at the top of a mountain, and yet these vents originated towards the center of the earth. Finally, as we approached the foot of the summit, we saw two climbers coming down from the top. It was 11:45 am. We reached the summit at about noon, and Vance and Mark were there to greet us. As it was a lovely clear day, the views of Lassen and Shastina were spectacular. "We made it!" said Deborah as she hugged Adrian. You could see the sense of relief and accomplishment on the faces of Vance and Mark as well. Soon after, we were joined by Melissa, Andrew, and Brian B. They said Carey and Brien were waiting for us below Misery Hill, opting not to go on ahead. Andrew wasn't looking too good but was elated to be at the summit. We took the obligatory summit photos and signed the logbook, all the while strategizing how we would get down the treacherously steep slopes we had climbed. Andrew was swaying and not feeling well, so we roped him up with Melissa and Mark.

It was surprisingly hot on the descent with the sun beating down on us, and we all stripped down to as little clothing as we could modestly muster. We had decided to take an alternate route through Avalanche Gulch which would be steep but more direct, and it would be possible to glissade through parts. Glissading entails sliding down the ice on your side, using your ice axe as a brake. It takes a fair amount of energy to keep yourself in control by digging your axe into the snow, but it was preferable to walking. For safety reasons, it is best to remove crampons while glissading so as not to catch on rock or ice and seriously injure yourself. It is an exhilarating way to get downhill, but it is hard on your pants, which usually end up with tears or holes, which is why most photos of Deborah's snow pants contain patches of duct tape. At the bottom of the slide we found ourselves at Helen Lake whereupon we traversed northwest for a mile or so to our campsite on the saddle.

We arrived at camp, elated and exhausted, and lazed around the tents in the sun. Heeding the endless need to melt snow for water we soon fired up the stoves, so we would have enough for our bottles and our "just add boiling water" meals. As usual, Carey took charge of the interminable task of watching the stoves, adding snow and decanting the precious water as it melted. Vance had been wearing light shoes with over-boots and as he

Brian B at red banks on the descent of Mount Shasta.

worked on his sore feet Adrian commented on his unusual choice of footwear for this mountain. 'This is nothing' he replied and told us how, among his more unusual talents, he is a skilled unicyclist, and has often performed in parades riding in a clown suit. That story led on to how, in order to better relate to his patients, he has competed in several marathons with a wheelchair or a handcrank bike.

Exhausted after reaching the summit, Deborah really was not hungry but when her need to eat returned, we discovered the ravens had visited our camp and taken more food! By Sunday night we had also run out of most of our hot meals, and were relying on snack foods and various odds and ends.

Since our tent had gone with Derek and Ray, Adrian and Deb slept in Brien's big 3-person expedition tent with Brien and Mark. Yes, that is four people crammed into a 3-person tent, a bit like matches in a box, but very warm. It always amazed Adrian that you could stay reasonably comfortable in 10-degree weather if you are moving or are sleeping in a tent with a suitable sleeping bag. The only time it was truly cold was when we took breaks from climbing or had to remove gloves to light the stove.

Notoriously a poor sleeper while camping, she had to get up and pee about 5 times that night! The next morning we left for our vehicles at Bunny Flat. After about a third of the way down, Ray came up to meet Deborah as she was once again fixing her crampon. She asked Ray what he was doing there and he said "to switch packs with you," and threw down his tiny fanny pack. She protested that it was not necessary and she could make it down the mountain with her humongous pack, but honestly, when someone really wants to do Deborah a favor, she has a hard time turning them down. The best part was that she arrived in the parking lot with everyone else, instead of them having to wait an hour. After returning our rented boots at the '5th Season' gear store, we all met up at Burger Express for one last meal before the long drive home. "Okay, Adrian, what's our next adventure?" Deborah asked. She knew some of the adventure racers in our group, notably Melissa and Mark, were going to do a race in Baja in a month, but she was really interested in more mountains. Adrian mentioned that he had always wanted to climb all the 14ers in California, and forgetting her promise not to climb more mountains Deborah agreed that sounded like a great idea. After all, what could be harder than what she had already accomplished? Little did she know...

Mount Sill.

Chapter 2
MT SILL

14,154 feet
July 30 - August 3, 2008
Summary: Success on Mt. Sill and an attempt on Polemonium Peak. The moral of this trip? Always carry a two-way radio.
Our Team: Adrian Crane, Ray Kablanow, Mark Richardson, and Deborah Steinberg. We were joined for part of the way by Lewis Ase, his girlfriend Carrie Pivcevich, and their dog Bruno.

We had originally planned to climb North Palisade and Thunderbolt Peak in the Palisades Range, but a last-minute strategic decision was made to leave these two much more difficult peaks until later. Instead, we decided to attempt Mt. Sill and nearby Polemonium Peak. The breathtaking Palisades Range is southwest of the town of Bishop and presents the greatest challenges of all the 14,000 ft peaks in California. The Palisades are characterized by arduously steep ascents and descents, proclivity for rockfalls, sharp cliffs, nasty talus, and melting glaciers - all which contribute to the challenge and thrill of success!

Thursday morning, we picked up a wilderness permit, did some last-minute shopping at the mountain shop in Bishop, finished packing gear in our backpacks, and set off at about 10:45 am from Big Pine Creek Trailhead for North Fork. It was decided that since Mark was the strongest one, we would give him most of the weight. Mark is a firefighter and athlete and exudes competence, the kind of guy you want around in case of emergency. His medical training is an always welcome asset on a wilderness trip. He is used to carrying hoses up tall buildings so we handed him our enormous 4-person tent, while Ray and Adrian each carried a bear canister full of our food. Deborah wanted to unload some of her other gear onto the guys, like her ice axe and crampons, but didn't have the heart. We met up with Lewis and Carrie, two uber-fit friends of ours, and set off at a very brisk pace. After a while we stopped for a water break and just as we were patting ourselves on the back for our amazing progress over the last three miles, we discovered the loaner boots Mark was wearing were delaminating at the heel. However, just prior to our discovery, Lewis and Carrie and their dog set off without a radio at super-speed pace towards our intended camp at Sam Mack Meadow (about 11,000 feet elevation), about a mile south and 500 feet higher than Third Lake. Knowing there happened to be another pair of boots in our vehicle, Mark dropped his pack and ran back to Ray's van. In the meantime, parts of his pack were re-distributed amongst Deborah, Ray, and Adrian, and the guys took turns piggybacking the pack onto their own pack. So much for our plan to have Mark carry all the weight!

Approach to Sill, the numbered lakes.

From that point forward, we all moved pretty slowly up the trail, and the four of us finally re-grouped at the fork of Black Lake trail and Numbered Lakes trail. We all wanted to give Mark a hard time about making us carry all this extra weight, but he looked pretty tired after hiking a rather brisk extra eight miles, so we kept our thoughts to ourselves. Lakes 1 through 3 were a chain of beautiful opaque turquoise lakes, filled with glacial flour and mountain water. We stopped to admire the views and take some photos. We finally arrived at Sam Mack Meadow at 5:45 pm, at least a couple hours behind Lewis and Carrie, and set up camp. Sam Mack Meadow was a narrow green patch bordered by rocky slopes and divided by a shallow but wide stream.

In lieu of technical responsibilities, Deborah had been put in charge of procuring food for our trip. She had been instructed multiple times before the trip to purchase very lightweight food by Ray, who, on a prep trip three weeks prior, had been relegated to carrying a block of Swiss cheese and a whole container of peanut butter. After our Mountain House "add-hot-water" meals had been consumed, Mark broke out the Gran Marnier, and Adrian was first in line with his cup. We laid out our strategy for the next day's summit attempt and set our alarms for 4:30 am. Adrian felt confident that the summit would not be too challenging, since he had remembered climbing it 15 years earlier without too much difficulty. Unfortunately, no one slept well because our slumber was punctuated by the sound of what was either thunderstorms or distant rock falls. This debate continued well into the next day as we witnessed two impressive rock falls near the glacier, but were reminded of the frequent thunderstorms that occur in the Eastern Sierras. We started out with our summit packs towards Mt. Sill with only 1 ½ liters of water apiece, deciding that we should be able to pick up glacial melt streams along the way. Unfortunately, once on the glacial moraines, we saw no chance of water, and had to descend a very steep loose rocky moraine to reach the lake at the toe of Palisade Glacier. Most of the rocks in this area were large, loose, and treacherous. We could see that many of the rocks had recently moved or fallen, and they shifted again as we stepped on them. They were big enough to easily trap a foot or break a leg. Spooked, Lewis, Carrie, and their dog headed back to camp.

Attempting to avoid as much talus as possible, we climbed the wide arc of older moraine rock around the northwest side of the lake and headed up towards the Palisade Glacier.

Interesting conversation abounds in difficult terrain. Ray, Mark, and Adrian debated the benefits of different energy foods for athletes such as Gu, NUUN, and Shot Blocks. Meanwhile, Deborah broke out the Oreos, which she whole-heartedly asserted to be the best low-tech energy food for ascending steep rocky gullies. Now well above 12,000 feet, it was decided that we were to take everyone's word with a grain of salt since the altitude was getting to us. With a view of Birch Mountain in the distance, we laughed about the fact that Deborah must definitely not be a princess to be out in this territory, but can occasionally be a real "birch." Eventually, we reached a point in the route where it appeared that we would have to traverse the vertically exposed north face of Mount Sill. We all took a collective gasp at the sight of the face, debating whether we were over our heads with this climb. Adrian surprised the group by saying none of this looked remotely familiar from his last attempt of this mountain, and he was not actually sure which way we should go next. He even started to doubt that he had really climbed Sill before, and not some other mountain. Eventually, we scouted out a route that, although precarious in places, was doable with rope on the exposed sections. In her head, Deborah debated the merits of being a princess instead of being out here where she had to consciously not look down. On the way, Adrian dropped his trekking pole, which we all watched as it bounced down 100 vertical feet into the gully. Finally, we managed to reach the Summit of Mt. Sill at 11:45 am. Looking around, Adrian stated "Oh yes, this looks familiar, I did climb this mountain before".

Ray on the Palisade Glacier

Before we left for our trip, we had decided that on each summit we would recognize someone's personal struggle with cancer by bringing along a tiny memento of the person we were recognizing. With that in mind, Deb signed the Summit Log, which was the first entry in five days, and left Kristin Machado's St. Mary medal, Richard Barasch's airline ticket, and a STOP CANCER pin in the Summit Box. We ate a lunch of very lightweight (but tasteless) cheese & cracker sandwiches and dried fruit and were joined by a solitary climber on his way from the south side of Sill. We read the guidebook and debated for 20 minutes which peak in our view was actually Polemonium, since some of our Google maps were unfortunately incorrect.

At 12:45, we left the summit of Mt. Sill and descended the talus towards the tiny Polemonium Glacier. As we slogged up-glacier, most of us were dragging and feeling tired except Deb who had been eating Oreos. Mark stopped and mentioned he was actually not feeling well and Deborah, having a feeling he was headed for a "bonk," offered him some Oreos. As he accepted the cookie the look on his face, somewhere between disgust and resignation, was priceless. At 3:30 pm, we were standing at 14,000 feet on top of Polemonium's false summit and were staring across a gully between us and the steep exposed spire that is Polemonium Peak, a mere 100 vertical feet away. Deciding that this was no place to train in Class 5 rock climbing, we vowed to take a clinic as a team and leave Polemonium Peak for another trip. So close, and yet so far!

On the summit of Sill. Adrian, Deborah, Ray, Mark.

We descended back to camp, scouting out better routes and rappelling down others. Deb was impressed with our navigational skills in the steadily decreasing light. Mark, usually a quiet guy anyway, would take a quick glance at the map, and point "this way" without much debate. We finally picked up a faint trail following cairns back to Sam Mack Meadow and arrived back at our campsite at 9:15 pm after 14 hours of climbing. We slept in Saturday morning, and Deb made the obligatory morning coffee. Again, Adrian was first in line with his cup out. We broke camp at 10 am Saturday morning and packed out. On our way back down, we arrived at a shady lunch spot where

Mark threw out his fishing pole and Ray and Adrian took a nap.

Just as were leaving, Deb announced she would catch up with everyone since she had to "use the facilities." After her short stop she set off down but accidentally left her trekking poles along the trail and, descending at a fast pace, passed the location where the guys were just off the path, pumping water and waiting for her. She headed down the trail more quickly, thinking that the reason the guys were so far ahead was the "horses smell the barn" effect and were rushing back to civilization. The guys finished filling the water bottles, and, with still no sign of Deborah, decided to search up and down the trail. Ray found her abandoned trekking poles and feared the worst. Thinking she had come across some awful fate in the woods, everyone spread out to find her, calling out 'Deborah! Deborah!'

Meanwhile, a mile and a half down the trail, Deborah realized that she forgot her trekking poles! She berated herself, thinking about how long the guys would have been waiting for her down at the van. She dropped her pack and broke into a run uphill in hiking boots with massive blisters on her feet. On the way, she ran into a solitary female hiker, who said, "Are you Deborah? Your three friends are looking for you." "Uh-oh." thought Deb. She finally reunited with Adrian, Ray, Mark, and her trekking poles and took a lot of manure from the guys about how she could possibly have missed them in such an obvious location 100 feet from her bathroom spot. Ray joked that she should wear an electronic shock collar should she ever wander that far off again. She replied that remembering to always carry a radio should suffice.

As we arrived back at the trailhead at 4:30 pm, Deborah realized she still had a few Oreos left, which were shared with the others. We then drove to Mammoth Lakes to meet up with a group of friends from Modesto who were at a Shadow Chase Running Club training camp and got hot showers at last! Deborah decided after a hot shower that being a princess is sometimes nicer than the alternative.

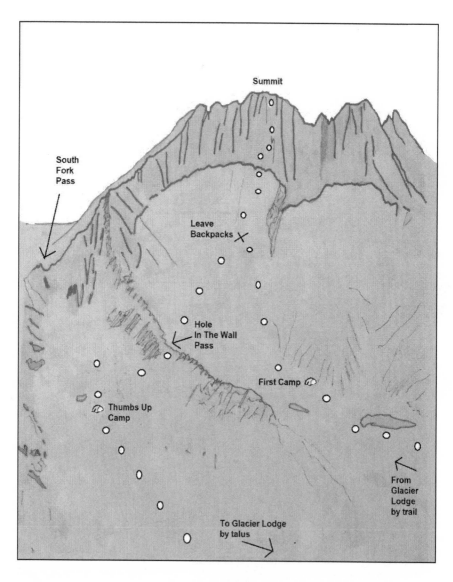

Summit

South
Fork
Pass

Leave
Backpacks ✕

Hole
In The Wall
Pass

First Camp

Thumbs Up
Camp

From
Glacier
Lodge
by trail

To Glacier Lodge
by talus

Middle Palisade.

Chapter 3
MIDDLE PALISADE

14,019 feet
September 10th - 14th, 2008
Summary: Success on Middle Palisade but never got near Split!
Our Team: Deborah Steinberg, Adrian Crane, Ray Kablanow, Christopher Crane and Rick Baraff.

Little did we know when we packed up our hiking boots, crampons, ice axes, harnesses, and Oreos that this would be our most difficult climb to date. Middle Palisade Peak lies south of the main massif of the infamous Palisade range near Bishop, surrounded by glacial moraine and nasty rocky talus. The terrain is so rough and rocky that once we began hiking off-trail towards the mountain, we didn't see a patch of grass for two whole days. On our previous climb up Mt. Sill, the blisters on Deborah's feet looked like something from a horror movie, so on this trip she was armed with trail shoes, new boots, socks, insoles, Elasticon tape, hydrocolloid blister bandages, tincture of Benzoin, Vaseline and 10 pages from the "Preventing Blisters" section of *Fixing Your Feet* reduced on a copy machine to 4pt font.

We left Modesto Wednesday evening so that we could sleep by the side of the road at 7,000 ft and begin acclimatizing to the altitude. We noticed right away that the temperature would be noticeably cooler than our last trip 4 weeks ago, which was unfortunate for Deborah who brought her daughter's lightweight sleeping bag instead of her winter down bag. This trip was also different in that we brought along Rick Baraff to film our adventure. Rick is a professional videographer and adventure racer who was sent along by "Sutter Medical Foundation Cancer Report" to document our trip. You would think a 20-pound camera would slow him down a bit, but his exercise regimen included standing on a balance ball, so hopping from loose rock to shaky boulder with his camera equipment was not a problem for him.

At 11:30 am Thursday morning, we left Glacier Lodge and the Big Pine Creek Trailhead. For this trip, our strategy was to head up the South fork of

Big Pine Creek to a high camp Thursday evening, climb Middle Palisade Friday and then move our base camp 5 miles down the Sierra Crest to attempt Split Mountain from the West on Saturday or Sunday. Lofty goals, to be sure!

Hiking along the trail, we passed by Birch Mountain where Deborah posed for a photo-op, since on the last trip we decided that as she is not a princess, she must be a 'birch.' After reaching Brainerd Lake, we found we no longer had trail, and by 4:15 pm Thursday we had reached the fabulous clear green water of Finger Lake. At 6:45 pm, we made camp among the gravel just below Middle Palisade Glacier. Deb declared she was happy because, at least to this point, she had avoided any blisters.

Deborah, high on Middle Palisade

Although we awoke at 5:15 am, it was 7:10 before we had finished breaking camp and started climbing with full packs to the moraine of Middle Pal Glacier where we dropped off all but our summit packs and climbing gear. At this point we were well above 12,000 feet, and the conversation got pretty colorful. Rick told Deborah about a somewhat erotic dream he had about a former girlfriend, and, since Deborah was always happy to dole out advice, she interpreted the dream to mean Rick had unresolved issues about his life as a single guy.

As we approached the base of the Middle Palisade cliffs, we looked for the Class 3 rock route to begin the climb above the glacier. We spent a full hour consulting our copied pages, with photos, from our guide book: *Climbing California's Fourteeners* by Porcella and Burns. We just could not see a reasonable way to start up the rock. Deborah felt the time was appropriate to turn on full "birch" mode. She declared that she would take a nap and not move until we found our route-- which we better find, "or else." Eventually we realized that what was confusing our efforts was that the snow level was significantly lower than what was shown in the 10+ year-old photo in the book. Ray finally found our route.

On the summit of Middle Palisade. Deborah, Ray, Rick, Adrian, Christopher

We sent Adrian's son Christopher, up 20 feet of treacherous climbing, belaying him from below, so that he could belay the rest of us from above to safety. Deborah thought it wise not to photograph the evidence for Adrian's wife Karen, should she really put the screws on. However, Adrian had full confidence in Christopher who had just finished working the summer at Camp Bruin Wood's Rope Course in the Angeles Mountains. After this short sketchy section, we climbed mostly without ropes for two hours, dodging small rocks, until we reached two spires which looked like they might be our summit. We had to decide which spire was the actual summit and which was a false impersonator. Finally, Rick picked what he thought was the actual summit, which required rope to ascend. We were much relieved to find a summit canister! The last log was only 2 days prior. Adrian signed the summit log as Deborah placed her mementos in the canister: a photo of her mother-in-law Nawatha Redding, who passed away from Lymphoma in 1998 and a Hebrew prayer scroll from her friend Andra Greenwald who just finished treatments for thyroid cancer that year. Andra also gave Deborah an extra scroll to carry on climbs for the rest of our trips, since the prayer contains the "Shma," thought to be a prayer of protection.

Counting on her "Shma" for security, Deborah rappelled 50 feet off the summit, then slowly descended on foot, frequently dislodging rocks downhill. Out of the blue, we heard a rock bouncing from above, and Adrian and Deb crouched down to make a small target. The rock hit Adrian and bounced across to Deb before continuing its trajectory into the void below. "Ow that hurt!" Deb shouted. "Oh, it can't have been that bad, it hit me first" responded Adrian. "Well it hit me in the neck" Deborah retorted. Adrian replied, "Well, you are lucky I absorbed most of the impact," brushing off her complaint. Back at camp, Adrian found that not only had his backpack cushioned the blow of the rock, but the Nalgene water bottle in the side pocket had been smashed by the rock, which takes a considerable impact to do. Adrian felt at once fortunate that the water bottle and pack had shielded him and apologetic to Deborah for ignoring her distress when the rock did hit her. Fortunately, the water bottle had taken the brunt of the force, but it reminded us all not to take our safety for granted. As it happened, we had been wearing helmets in that section, but that was rare for us. As we learned firsthand the risks of rockfall in these loose eroding mountains, we became more diligent in wearing helmets whenever the going got steep.

We finished the climb by rappelling off the last step to the glacier. A short but slow descent over the moraine returned us to the gear we had left behind earlier. Now with heavy backpacks, we set off towards our intended camp 5 miles away. While planning the trip back home, it had seemed that a stroll along some trail through green flower-filled valleys would bring little hardship. But ahead, on our quest for Split Mountain, we could see only gruesome talus and an exceedingly steep rocky pass. Jumping from huge rock to huge rock is tiring without a backpack, and we had our full camp in our backpacks. By 6 pm, we were exhausted and had made it up to "Hole in the Wall" pass where we rested and looked ahead to "South Fork Pass." To our dismay, South Fork Pass was another mile of huge talus blocks and then one-thousand vertical feet of steep, loose scree above a glacial moraine. We looked at each other in unison, and, after several unprintable comments regarding our enthusiasm at climbing that pass with 60-pound backpacks at the end of the day, agreed that the public comment would be "no way."

We descended talus into the midst of the glacial moraine. As dusk fell, we found ourselves with no choice but to camp on the rubble and rock of the glacier. There was nothing flat, and it was quite possibly the worst choice for a campsite that we had ever seen. We came across a vague bowl filled with medium-sized rocks and decided to make the best of it. When asked by Ray if this was camp, Christopher and Adrian turned and gave an unenthusiastic thumbs up sign, hence the name "Thumbs Up Camp."

Christopher and Adrian celebrate the finding of 'thumbs up' camp.

They were sure they would be able to hack a tent platform from the rock garden. Even though our camp was primitive, to say the least, Deb was in good spirits. She had avoided the blisters that had so plagued her on earlier trips because she had taken Mark's advice to read John Vonhof's book *Fixing Your Feet*. Ray and Christopher rolled and wrestled the rocks to create a vague semblance of flatness and put up the tent. Rick found a large almost flat topped rock and pitched his one person tent on the top, creating a reasonable sleeping place. Unimpressed by the guys' work on our tent, Deb wandered over to ask if maybe she could squeeze in with Rick. She returned, disappointed to her fate in the rocky four-person tent. Christopher was sent down to retrieve water from the glacial lake below that was surrounded by ice walls. Meanwhile, Deborah proceeded to help with dinner, and, failing to remove one of the protective plastic covers, ended up melting part of Ray's brand new Jet Boil. After a disconcertingly long period of time, Christopher struggled back to camp with a haul of bottles, very cold hands, and stories of "by the fingernails" holds on the ice as he stretched a bottle down into the freezing waters to fill it. With the smell of plastic punctuating our dinner, Deborah took a good-natured berating on how someone with two university degrees and many nights camping could still not properly use a stove.

Christopher and Ray enjoy 'thumbs up' camp

That night, sleeping tight in the four-person tent, each perso with their own personal boulder problem. During that long unc night attempting to sleep on our rocks, we heard the loud crash of and rocks falling into the glacial lake below.

The next morning Ray looked anything but rested. He described the place in his designated corner of the tent as "a rock in the middle with a hole at each end", which he filled with gear to make a semblance of flatness. The rest of us envied Adrian who looked completely awake and refreshed as if he had spent the night sleeping at the Hilton. Fortunately for Adrian, he has the remarkable talent of being able to fall asleep in thirty seconds or less, even if he lies down next to a freeway. Most of us were still a bit groggy as we enjoyed our morning coffee, and we discussed our strategy to return to the trailhead, recover, and think about climbing Split on Sunday. As it turned out, the morning was miserable. We meandered down through granite ledges and jagged talus with several dead ends involved. Thoughts of mutiny started to trickle into all but the hardiest souls. Deborah started cursing as she struggled to maintain composure after falling for the umpteenth time on all the loose rocks and boulders. Ray, ever the calm one, tried to distract her with a story that would keep her from strangling Adrian.

Finally, at 1:30 pm we regained the main trail. Deb realized that although every other part of her hurt, her feet felt fine. About two miles from the trailhead, she forgot her trekking poles AGAIN, which fortunately was immediately discovered by Adrian and Christopher, who gave her another good-natured, but well-deserved, scolding. Deb then tried to distract our thoughts with ideas for homing devices for her trekking poles. Eventually, we reached our vehicle and realized that, in order to summit Split Peak the next day, we would have to climb 7,000 vertical feet up and then down in one day from another trail head. Adrian, of course, was all for it. After much animated discussion, it was decided that, in order to preserve our friendship and thus achieve our goal of summiting all the California 14ers, we needed to plan on attempting only one summit per trip. So, our plans for Split Peak were aborted. With no hard feelings, we ate a fabulous dinner in Bishop, and reminisced what a great trip it was. Deb declared that the five of us are hardy souls.

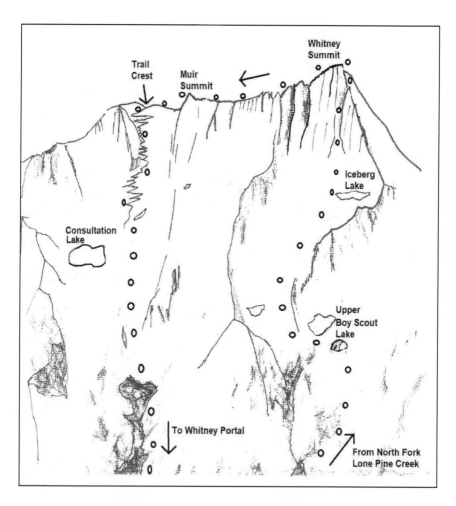

Mount Whitney and Mount Muir.

Chapter 4
MT WHITNEY AND MT MUIR

14,505 feet (Mt. Whitney) and 14,150 (Mt. Muir)
November 20th - 23rd, 2008
Summary: Cold weather success on Whitney (via Mountaineer's Route) and Muir. Also known as the "est" trip.
Our Team: Adrian Crane, Deborah Steinberg, Ray Kablanow, Derek Castle, Carey Gregg and Rudolphe Jourdaine.

After our exhausting climb of Middle Palisade Peak, we began to wonder just how extreme was the nature of our endeavor to climb all of the California 14ers. Was it destined to be a grueling and draining challenge? We had originally planned to climb two 14ers on that trip (Split Mountain along with Middle Palisade), but were stymied by the size and difficulty of a mountain pass that looked much easier on the map. At the end of our trip, we had decided to climb only one summit per trip. However, that resolution did not last long, and we had already made an exception on this trip. Since Muir Peak is just so close to Whitney, we had to attempt it if conditions were good. Mt. Whitney is the highest peak in California, but it can also be the easiest with a nice trail all the way up to the top. True to his nature, Adrian decided to up the challenge a bit, so our plan was to set off in November up the alternative Mountaineer's route. As it turned out, our weather was wonderful, although quite cold with temperatures dropping to the mid teens overnight. If we were lucky enough to be climbing with the sun upon us, the temperature would climb to around 50 degrees. To stay warm, we had to keep moving, and our breaks were necessarily brief.

Friday morning, everyone pulled their packs out of Ray's van with their gear already neatly packed, except Adrian who, as per usual, pulled out an empty backpack and a full-to-the-brim gear bag and proceeded to sort all his gear in the parking lot. He started to worry that he would earn his reputation as the guy that is always the last one ready until he remembered that it takes Deborah 20 minutes to prep her feet with blister prevention pads and tapes!

At 10 am, with the obligatory permits and WAG bags in our possession, we set out for our base camp at Upper Boy Scout Lake along the mountaineering route to Mt. Whitney.

Adrian pauses by a frozen waterfall on Lone Pine Creek.

There are a few mountains, most notably Whitney, Shasta, and Rainier, where WAGS waste bags are required due to the large volume of people climbing the mountain. In order for the mountain not to become one heaping toilet, you are required to pack out everything, including your poop and toilet paper. The reason behind this is that, although the mountain is large, the majority of people travel along the same route. Fortunately, by double-bagging everything in zip bags there is no odor, and the whole thing can be dumped in a special receptacle at the trailhead when you return.

Since we knew we were going to attempt Muir Peak on Saturday along with Whitney, the sensible thing to do would have been to walk up the main trail, a traditional switchback route up the mountain, and set up camp along the way there. However, several in the group had their heart set on the more challenging mountaineering route, which meant that our timing on summit day was critical if we didn't want to descend the more treacherous parts of the mountain in the dark. On the way to our base camp, we enjoyed the beautiful winter conditions of powdery snow, gorgeous natural water fountains, the bluish tinge of iced-over waterfalls, and clear blue sky. One frozen waterfall we passed looked like a giant fairy wedding cake that was as large as an Olympic-sized pool, its ice crystals glistening in the sun. Early on, Deborah lost her camera while bushwhacking in the dense alder along the stream. It was only later that we learned about the more technical "Ridge Route" that allows you to avoid the brush. One advantage of climbing Whitney in off-season is that you don't have nearly as many people on the mountain, and you don't have to deal with the lottery process to get your climbing permits. As it turned out, when we arrived at Upper Boy Scout Camp there was only one other climbing party there, a group of college students celebrating the 21st birthday of one of their members.

Although the climb to base camp was slow and steady, our altimeters read 11,300 feet and Carey and Rudolphe were suffering from mild Altitude Sickness by the time we reached camp at 4 pm on Friday. Altitude Sickness, or Acute Mountain Sickness, is common above 8,000 feet, and some people are more susceptible than others. Mild Altitude Sickness is not dangerous, and includes headache, nausea, and trouble sleeping. However, if someone's breathing sounds like a paper bag crumpling, that is a sign of a more serious problem that requires immediate attention and a quick descent if possible. Altitude Sickness is often successfully treated with Acetazolamide, and many people bring that medication on mountaineering trips. Carey and Rudolphe didn't feel well enough to make a bid for the summit, but since they felt it was not serious enough to descend they volunteered to stay in camp. This meant that only Adrian, Deborah, Ray, and Derek left at 6 am Saturday morning to attempt Mt. Whitney and Muir.

We set off towards the northeast side of the mountain following mostly good trail, and Deb had the feeling that this was all going along much too easily. Adrian must have been feeling bored, because eventually we came to a large rocky bluff that we had to either climb up and over (the "macho route") or climb down toward a trail along the valley floor (the "weenie route"). Naturally Deb wanted to take the "weenie route," but Adrian decided we should climb up the icy rocks and around scary ledges of the bluff. Once over the bluff, we arrived at the foot of the mountaineer's route, a steep snow gully below "the notch" of the mountain. Once our crampons were on securely, we roped up together and slogged up the mountain for nearly an hour and a half. Once at the top of the ridge, we stopped to rest briefly, but realized we were so cold that stopping for long was not an option.

We crossed the Sierra Crest to the west side and traversed west then south, where eventually we joined up with the traditional walk-up Whitney trail and hiked the last quarter mile to the summit, where we radioed Carey of our success. We brought two mementos to the top to drop into the summit box for STOP CANCER: Adrian brought a photo in memory of his brother Christopher, and Deborah brought a penny in honor of Harriette Kirschen.

Harriette and Morrie Kirschen tutored Deborah's daughters for their Bat Mitzvahs, and at the end of each session there would be a vocabulary quiz, in which a penny was earned for each word translated correctly. Harriette was also known for making delicious brownies for the students, but that would have been a more difficult item to put in the summit box, so we ate some in her honor! As we signed the summit log, we realized that we were the first group that day to reach the top of Whitney. We found out later that we were also the only group to use the "Mountaineer's Route" to reach the summit that day. Unfortunately, once Deb reached the summit she was "done" and had absolutely no motivation to climb Muir Peak. It took a lot of cajoling from Adrian, Derek, and Ray, a little rest, and more than a few Oreos to convince her that climbing Muir today would save her a trip up the mountain another day.

Adrian on the Climber's Route of Mount Whitney.

Fortunately, the route to Muir was a mere mile down the trail from Whitney's summit and needed only 500 vertical feet of climbing above the trail. Derek was pretty tired at this point and decided to wait for us where we left the trail. Muir, at 14,150 feet, is less well-known than its more famous neighbor but was a quick exciting scramble to the top. We did actually have to rope up at the end for a small section of Class 4 scrambling, but it was a rather fun peak. With Whitney and Muir behind us, our California 14er total came to 5 down, 10 to go!

Deborah on the summit of Mount Whitney

By the time we had climbed down the summit rocks and descended the talus back to the trail it was 4 pm. Time was critical as at this time of year it would be dark soon after five. Adrian and Derek worried that we would be climbing the more precarious traverses across Whitney in the dark if we went back the way we came, so it was decided we should travel down the traditional Whitney trail to a point where we could cut cross-country to our base camp.

When we arrived at Trail Crest it was almost 5 pm, and Adrian, Derek, and Ray took a look at our route in the last of the daylight. From our high viewpoint we could see the section where we would be traveling cross-country. Compared to how it appeared on the map, it seemed a lot less feasible in reality as we saw how steep an intervening ridge appeared to be, especially since we would be trekking with headlamps in the dark. Our only remaining safe option was to trek down the traditional Whitney trail 9 miles in the dark all the way to our vehicle at Whitney Portal. The switchbacks from Trail Crest descended 2000 very icy feet to the Trail Camp area, and from there we continued by headlamp along the snowed-over trail. Eventually, as our altitude lessened, the snow cover became less and, apart from icy patches to catch the unwary, the trail was mostly good. We arrived at our van at 11 pm, exhausted. Unfortunately, our sleeping bags were at base camp as were Carey and Rudolphe who would be wondering what had happened to us. Lucky for us, Ray's Sportmobile does not need to run all night to run the heater, so we had no problem keeping warm. "The Beast," as it is often called, is a large camper van that sleeps four comfortably and is often the perfect vehicle for our adventures since it includes running water, a refrigerator, and a microwave. Wherever we stopped to get diesel, complete strangers would flock to the Sportsmobile and ask questions. Ray would politely entertain an audience with his fans for a few minutes in his cool and calm way and then feign the need to reach our destination quickly so that he would not be permanently delayed. Ray's van makes him a popular guy on any kind of adventure, but he has known us long enough to know that we would like him even if he didn't own such a fabulous vehicle.

Deborah with Ray above, nearing the summit of Mt Muir.

Ray is a quiet guy, remarkably lean and fit for a guy in his sixties and a geologist by trade, frequently doing field work for various environmental and water projects. He is probably the most soft-spoken member of our group, and is a definite weather-nerd, checking multiple sites before each trip. Even though he currently has long curly hair bound in a ponytail, he was raised in an observant Adventist family, and was not exposed to television or rock n' roll during his youth. We like to joke that Ray has "Culture Deficit Disorder," and may be one of the few people his age who cannot name all four Beatles. His political affinities and penchant for guns differ from some other members of the group, but any political discussions we have are always respectful, and it is remarkable that we rarely have hurt feelings. Ray committed to climbing all the California 14ers as well, and his goal was to raise funds for The Howard Training Center, an activity center for the developmentally disabled in the Modesto area.

Now inside the van, the four of us quickly pushed our gear out of the way, and were sawing logs as soon as we managed to lie down.

Although we tried several times, we had not been able to reach Carey by radio since the Whitney summit, and we still needed to retrieve our gear at base camp. So the next morning we set out once again along the mountaineering route toward Carey and Rudolphe. Carey had the good sense to hike up to a promontory where, amazingly, he was able to reach us by radio at about 7:30 am. Relief was evident in his voice as we told him what had happened and that we would be arriving there soon. By the time we reached camp at 10:20 am, Carey and Rudolphe had packed up most of the gear. In about 30 minutes, we were once again traveling down the mountain, with our packs, toward the van. The ice and snow that we had easily trekked across on the way up was feeling a little more treacherous going downhill especially since Deborah's crampons were now in the van. Fortuitously, Derek found a pair of crampons on the trail, like manna from heaven! We arrived back at our vehicle at Whitney Portal at 2pm, feeling fortunate that all had gone so well. Deborah declared that the theme for this trip was "est": we had the longest summit day; it was our coldest climb so far; it was our easiest climb from a technical standpoint (with a few exceptions); and we had by far the prettiest views of all our climbs to this point. On the drive back we discussed our strategies for climbing the rest of the California 14ers.

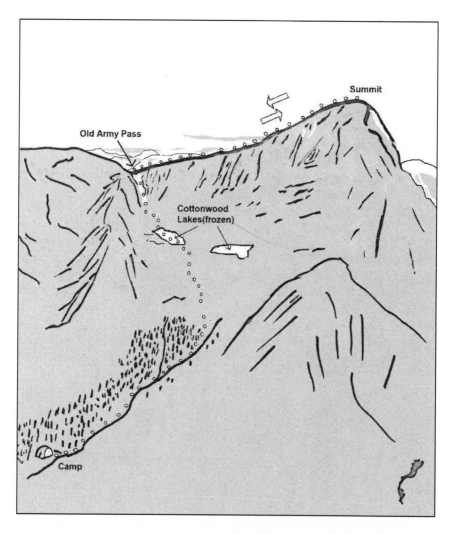

Mount Langley.

Chapter 5
LANGLEY IN WINTER

14,026 feet
March 13th - 15th, 2009
Summary: Victory snatched from the Jaws of Defeat on Langley.
Our Team: Adrian Crane, Deborah Steinberg, Ray Kablanow, Carey Gregg.

Whenever a trip seems quick and easy on paper, you can leave it to Adrian to make sure there will be enough challenge in it. We knew from the beginning that this strictly winter-conditions climb would be less technical with a long approach. What we didn't know was that the very length of it would make us most doubtful of success. We knew that in winter we could not drive all the way to the trailhead but expected to make it near the snowline at 8,000 feet, three miles from the trailhead. Two days before leaving, we discovered that the road to the trailhead was actually closed 12 miles from the trailhead at 5600 feet. We scrambled to come up with a solution for those extra miles and decided on bicycles. So, we planned to ride, with full backpacks, 12 miles uphill – not an inviting prospect!

When we arrived Thursday evening, we camped at the road closure. Ray disclosed that he had caught a cold three days prior, and was feeling under the weather. Fortunately, on Friday morning, with bikes laid out and ready to start our long ride, a rancher couple let us through their property with the van. Adrian was actually worried that we were not going to be able to use the bicycles at all, which would have made things too easy. However, snow and ice on the road and a lack of functioning 4WD allowed us to reduce our trek by only 5 ½ miles and 2200 feet in elevation gain, leaving us with plenty of enjoyable(!) riding. From there we rode our bikes uphill, walking them when necessary through the patches of snow. Carey pulled a kiddie trailer that was loaded down with 50 pounds of our heavier items, but we all still rode with full packs. It was a slow grind in lowest gear. Eventually, we reached a point where we were pushing our bikes through patches of snow more than riding them, so we ditched our bikes in full view on the side of the road, put on our snowshoes, and took off on foot. We were still a good 3 miles from the trailhead, and we figured the likelihood of anyone else being around to steal our bikes was pretty low.

Deborah riding toward Mount Langley

After a couple of miles, Adrian thought we should ditch our snowshoes, since he rarely ever needed them beyond 10,000 feet. Deb argued that if we need them and don't have them we will be up a creek without a paddle, and we were still slogging through quite a bit of snow. That turned out to be the call of the day, because we ended up on snowshoes most of our trip. Traveling on snowshoes is a bit like hiking in sand. Just as there are many types of sand, there are numerous types of snow, which affects how difficult it will be to trek through. It is extremely difficult to break trail in heavy wet snow, but cold dry fluffy snow or, better yet, hard compacted snow is much easier. Over many miles of terrain, you are likely to see all types and levels of difficulty. One thing is for sure: travel by snowshoe on soft snow is much more tiring than travel on hard ice or snow with crampons. Crampons grab the hard ice like cleats on a grassy hill while snowshoes still sink into the soft snow. Since crampons were not an option at this point, we had to continue on our snowshoes, laboriously navigating our way towards Langley. Adrian and Ray took turns breaking trail. We knew that the more progress we made today, the more likely we were to summit the next day. Although we were not nearly as far as we had hoped by 5:30 pm, we found two large downed trees and set up camp between them, giving ourselves space on the logs for our kitchen. Our elevation was 10,200 feet. Carey quickly set in to melt snow for water for our dehydrated meals and drinks. Now stopped, we soon felt increasingly cold as the temperature dropped with the sun. As we set up the tent with numb fingers and threw in our sleeping gear everyone became jealous when they saw Carey's new down-filled sleeping pad.

Ray and Deborah on Cottonwood Lakes heading toward Old Army Pass.

We woke at 5:30 am Saturday morning to frozen hiking boots. In fact, anything that did not sleep with us in our sleeping bags overnight was frozen. It took us a while to choke down some instant oatmeal and attend to business, so we did not set off on snowshoes that morning until 7:00 am. The terrain was incredibly beautiful, and we were amazed at all the trees and evidence of wildlife present at such high elevation. The tree line was at almost 11,000 ft, and we saw the tracks of rabbit, bear, and coyote crossing our snowshoe path.

A few hours later, Deb was snowshoeing behind Ray and wondering why his pace was so slow. Thinking that maybe his cold was getting to him, she took over breaking trail and realized that the reason Ray was moving so slowly is that breaking trail is exhausting and slow work. Deb lasted about 100 yards and then spent the next two hours apologizing. Adrian worried that we were not moving at a fast enough pace, so Deb encouraged him to be in the lead since he is usually amazingly strong in the snow. He moved ahead to share duties. Feeling fatigued from the long day before, Carey decided to head back to camp and be support crew.

Deborah and Ray climb Old Army Pass

Carey's the kind of guy you want on any adventure, despite his tendency towards altitude sickness. He is kind and hardworking, and will thoughtfully move out of hearing distance when he has to throw up. He owns an auto shop, but when Deb first met him she thought he was an engineer because of his attention to detail. Carey volunteers for several groups, including the local running club and Gold Rush Adventure Racing and is always the one assigned to loading and unloading heavy equipment at 4 am, a thankless job. He never really asks what he can do, he just sets about doing whatever he thinks needs to get done, like melting snow for water or shoveling snow to create a flat space for camp and kitchen. He likes to entertain us with off-color jokes, and even when he is puking from the altitude he swears that he really enjoys all these mountain adventures. Well into his sixties and amazingly fit, you would never know that he was a pot dealer in his youth.

After some scrapes with the law and after he and his family were robbed at gunpoint in their home, he realized this was not the future he wanted to have, and he turned his life around without looking back. We are grateful to have him among our friends.

Eventually, our group, now numbering three, reached Lower and Upper Cottonwood Lakes which was an eerily beautiful frozen open space. The lakes were covered in a layer of frosty snow that looked like someone had spread royal icing sprinkled with a sparkly diamond dust. We traded our snowshoes for crampons and laughed that to those watching us on SPOT satellite tracking it would look like we were swimming across the lake, since the satellite photos Google Earth uses are from summer. So late it was in the day and only just now onto crampons, Adrian was sure that we were continuing only to save face and that the summit was out of reach. However, Deb was impressed that Ray was continuing to slog on despite his drippy nose and sore throat, although he was even more quiet than usual. In typical Ray-style, he was determined to suffer through it. At the far end of Upper Cottonwood Lake is Old Army Pass, a steep snow slope 500 vertical feet up at a 45 degree angle. We decided to rope up and not look down. For most of the pass we were kicking steps in the ice and ascending slowly but safely. Then, we found ourselves in a patch of hard blue ice where we were precariously hanging on by the tips of our crampon spikes and the picks of our ice axes, and we prayed that if we slipped our companions would have enough grip to keep us all from sliding downslope en masse. Deb panicked briefly but loudly as she slid down a patch of blue ice. After she finished freaking out, Deb looked back to find that Adrian and Ray had her secured on a few feet of rope with an ice axe buried to the hilt as a belay. Her legs continued to shake after the burst of adrenaline.

We reached the top of Old Army Pass at noon. Since, according to the map, Old Army Pass was the most difficult section of our climb, we started to have a feeling that it might be possible to make the summit by 4 pm, although that would still leave precious little time to descend the steeper sections safely in daylight. We were exhausted, but since Deb and Adrian were climbing for STOP CANCER and Ray was climbing for the Howard Training Center we were loath to give up. Deb started to get blisters on the bottom of her feet, but decided she didn't have the time to stop and fix them. After another rather steep climb we reached 13,000 feet elevation and saw fresh tracks in the snow from a herd of mountain goats. Amazed at the idea of wildlife living so high, we then ran across fox tracks as well. We traversed across an endless plateau and reached a false summit, only to realize the real summit was another half a mile away. We were exhilarated when we reached the true summit at 3:35 pm and were treated to outstanding views of snow-covered mountains on every side through the icy clean air. The 360-degree view of rocky peaks strewn with snow and ice was quite literally breathtaking, and we all agreed it was a spiritual moment. There was a bit of a haze far off in the distance to the South, which we surmised could be Los Angeles, yet we were all alone. We quickly took photos and video, signed the log book, and took a moment to remember Barbara Carnes, Adrian's sister-in-law who died of lung cancer in 2003. We also climbed in honor of Crystal Franco, Deborah's co-worker at the time, who battled breast cancer. We took some pride in the fact that the last log in the summit book was from two months prior! We put our mementos in the summit box and began descending.

Adrian and Deborah celebrate on the summit of Langley

The long high ridge we were descending was very exposed to the weather, and the wind began to rise. It came in sharp bursts and sometimes had the power to throw us all off balance. Luckily it was not until we were back at the top of Old Army Pass roping up for the descent that the real wind began to hammer us. We scampered over the edge and were suddenly into the relative shelter of the gully. Descending the steep snow took a long time and by the time we made it to the flat wastes of the lake it was dusk. We took a break to eat, remove our sunglasses, retrieve our snowshoes, and then find this morning's snowshoe trail before it got truly dark. Back into the trees, we were not entirely sheltered from the icy wind as we picked out our trail toward camp. In the noise of the crunching snowshoes, it was hard to carry on a conversation, so we each enjoyed our own thoughts in the dark woods and bright snow around us. Our progress was quick because the trail was already broken from our ascent earlier in the day, and was easy to follow as our headlamps would literally light up the broken snow like a fiber optic tube. We wasted no time during our return trek and radioed ahead to Carey who had hot water and dinner ready when we arrived back at camp at 10:15 pm. By 11:20 pm we were in our tent, and as usual, it took Adrian 20 seconds before he was fast asleep.

Sunday morning, we awoke at 7:30 am, and it took 20 minutes for Deb to prepare her feet for the day with blister pads and tape. Adrian got up to melt snow for water, and realized he was having difficulty seeing. He was a little unnerved, and mentioned it to Deborah, who happens to be an Optometrist. Just before Adrian started to panic that there was something really wrong with his eyes, Deborah realized he had grabbed the wrong pair of glasses from the tent. He swapped glasses with Carey and regained his vision! Apparent emergency over, we broke camp, and by 10:10 am we were back on the trail. We made good progress until we reached our bicycles and found the kiddie trailer which was to carry all our heavy gear had a flat tire. After much discussion about pumps and Schrader valves versus Presta valves we discovered the large hole in the tube. Not having a spare for the trailer tire, we decided that we would have to make a 26 inch tube for the bike fit into the 20 inch trailer tire. We stuffed the tube in folded and twisted and pumped it up. Miraculously it seemed to work, and at 1:30 pm we set off on the bikes. Downhill was much more successful on bikes and we reached the van at 2:00 pm. We realized that, despite how close we were to Southern California as the crow flies, we had seen no other people in 2 ½ days! Just a hundred miles away in the Los Angeles basin there are 10 million people, but here there were just us four. Our navigation during the 33-mile round trip was exclusively by map and compass, and we had no trails or signs to follow. Adrian felt like the suspense of not knowing whether we were going to make it made the success that much more appreciated. At dinner in Lone Pine we debated which climb so far had the most beautiful views, and we all decided that this trip was definitely up there near the top.

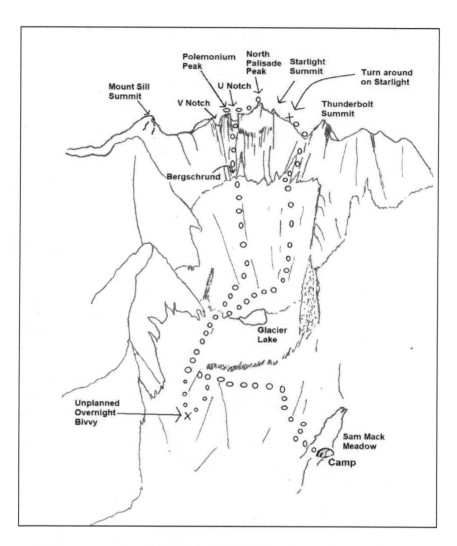

North Palisade and Polemonium Peak.

Chapter 6
NORTH PALISADE AND POLEMONIUM PEAK

14,249 feet (North Palisade) and 14,081 feet (Polemonium Peak) summits, and failed attempt of Starlight Peak
July 29th - August 2nd, 2009
Summary: Our first foray into the real Palisades
Our Team: Adrian Crane, Deborah Steinberg, Ray Kablanow, Ryan Swehla with assistance from Jack & John Styer on July 29.

This adventure had all the makings of a good drama: suspense, a wrong turn, a night out in the wilderness without tent or sleeping bags, and a few tears. It was another hard-won cache of memories from our efforts, and, although we had to take it all in stride, it does happen to make a really good story.

We left Modesto on Tuesday evening July 28, rushing off as soon as we had arrived home from work so that we could be at the trailhead near Bishop two hundred mountainous miles away in enough time to start acclimatizing overnight to the altitude. Once more at a diesel stop, Ray was distracted by admirers of the Sportsmobile, and we had to politely cut short the questions of his audience in order to keep us moving along on a timely schedule. We knew we had a long drive ahead of us.

On Wednesday morning at the trailhead after our usual sorting of gear, we were greeted by fellow Modestans Jack and John Styer, who had been backpacking and fishing at the "Numbered Lakes" area and who had been nice enough to pick up our permits for us at the Ranger Station. Furthermore, they arrived down the trail with nearly empty packs, so they could act as porters for our long trek into base camp at Sam Mack Meadow. Of course, the most grateful party member was Deborah. Although her pack was usually about the same weight as everyone else's, relative to her size it was by far the heaviest, making her almost always the slowest on the hike in. In addition, since we knew these to be more technical peaks, we had to carry in a lot more heavy climbing gear than usual.

Dark clouds filled the sky, and it started to rain intermittently as Deborah hiked behind Jack and listened to him tell fascinating stories of all his past adventures and occupations. Jack will often pace friends while they run hundred mile races and is a good cheerleader as well as an amazing long distance runner. When necessary, he can talk continuously for hours just to keep someone upright and moving. One time while he was out for a run, he ran out of trail and, instead of turning around, ended up scaling a cliff, and eventually ended up in someone's ritzy backyard, where he was greeted with a "May I help you?" For entertainment value, Jack makes a wonderful trail partner.

Another positive addition to this trip was Ryan Swehla. Considerably younger and taller than everyone else in the group, Deborah called him "The Viking." Ray knew him from Rotary, and as a former Eagle Scout from a very adventurous troop he was happy to join our quest to climb all of the California 14ers. Since scouting was high on Deborah's list of activities, she liked him immediately. Overall a self-assured and positive guy, he also had more rock climbing skills than the rest of us, which helped immensely during the more technical sections of our climb where he confidently took the lead.

We were all a bit soaked from the rain on the hike in. We arrived at Sam Mack Meadow (elevation 11,060 feet) by mid-afternoon and debated for some time whether to continue past the lush meadow for a higher base camp. It was decided that scenic beauty and easy access to water far outweighed any small savings in time for the next day by having a camp further up the trail. Wearing virtually no rain gear and having even less fat for warmth, Jack chilled quickly, so he and John left us for their camp at the lower lakes after big hugs from all of us for their enormous help getting us to base camp. While we set up our tent, we gazed up at the view of the Palisades and finalized our plans for the climb tomorrow. There are four difficult 14ers in the Palisades: North Palisade, Polemonium, Thunderbolt, and Starlight, and every route involves steep rock climbing or loose scrambling. To access the main ridge we would cross the Palisade Glacier and then climb the steep ice and snow of the U notch, a steep and striking gully in the center of the panorama that enables climbers to reach the ridgeline. Although not far apart in terms of miles, the connecting ridges and gullies are technical and difficult. Our first priority was to climb North Palisade and then we would get as many others as we could manage either tomorrow or in the following days.

After setting up camp in the bushes at the edge of the meadow, we saw someone at the creek and Deborah went down for a chat. She was the young guide for a team that had just returned with the "Beta" from the top of the U notch. Since this heavily-tattooed and pierced professional guide of their group was about 25 years younger than our average age, much of what she said was in a lingo that was unintelligible to Deborah, and even to Ryan who is 30. We were able to discern that we were supposed to stay to the right on the U-Notch to avoid the hard blue ice in the center and the "'schrund" or bergshrund, a deep Z-shaped crack at the foot of the snow gully where it connects with the glacier.

Crossing the Palisade glacier toward the U Notch.

After forcing ourselves to go to bed at 7 pm, we were awakened the next morning at 3:00 am by Ryan's watch alarm, all of us hoping the others had not heard it. The information we deciphered from the guide the previous day turned out to be quite helpful, making our ascent of the U-notch largely uneventful, with very little hard ice and mostly good kickable snow. We arrived at the top of the U-notch by 9:00 am feeling empowered that the rest of the climb to North Palisades Peak should be manageable and that attempting two summits in one day would allow us to avoid a return trip up the U-notch. However, after the U-notch, the real climbing began, and the next 50 vertical feet of the "Ryan variation of the Clyde variation of the Chimney Route" took us over 90 minutes to ascend.

Adrian and Deb on the Norman Clyde Variation

After more strenuous climbing, we finally reached the summit ridge and scrambled through the bowl to the final summit blocks.

The blocks are huge, and looking down through the gaps and cracks between them we were exposed to views of the Palisade Glacier 1000 feet below, evoking tears from Deborah as she had to leap across a few of them. Although she was securely tied in, she feared she would slam against the rocks before swinging into an abyss if she slipped. Deborah was relieved when we all made it to the summit unscathed despite the huge cracks leading to oblivion below. Once at the summit of North Palisade at 2:30 pm, we were able to relax and eat lunch in the lovely warm still air, basking in the knowledge we had just achieved summit number seven for Climb for a Cure. A glider buzzed by our heads and made several passes, waving as he went past. Deborah put two mementos in the summit box for two men who live with cancer: a Livestrong bracelet for Ed Blankenship and a portion of the Minarets map for Tom Gough, who had joined us on one of our earlier training trips. We spent an hour on top debating whether to attempt Polemonium or Starlight Peak next, while there still was time. We knew with a second summit attempt in one day we would be returning by headlamp, but it would be well worth avoiding a second climb of the U-notch and the nasty boulders and snowfield below.

We decided to climb Polemonium next, since we felt it was a better bet to summit. Since we came so close at our last attempt of it a year prior, we figured we knew the mountain better and were more likely to be successful than we would be with Starlight, which was a complete unknown. We down-climbed and rappelled to the top of the U-Notch by 5:30 pm. Since we wanted to be at the top of Polemonium and back to the U-Notch no later than 7:30 pm, so as to avoid the more treacherous sections in the dark, there was no time to spare. Ryan had been our lead climber for much of the trip, but Adrian tied in first for Polemonium and led a short but amazingly tricky class 5 pitch that lead to easier ground. We made surprising progress, and headed for a notch inside a gendarme to find an easy gully. At the top of the short gully, Adrian took a look at another Class 5 stretch and called Ryan forward to tackle it. Ryan easily led us up that bit, belaying the rest of us up once he was anchored. Then we pushed through a short scramble over more blocks to make it to the summit of Polemonium by 7:00 pm. This was summit number 8 for Climb for a Cure, and we were ecstatic to be over half way through the 15 fourteeners!

Quickly, we snapped pictures, signed the log book, and put our mementos in the Summit box of two beloved local teachers whose lives were cut short by cancer: Arlene Berry and Debbie Renz . We were still lucky to have good weather upon us, although the sky to the west looked threatening, and the sun was rapidly descending. We needed to rappel down three sections, and during the second rappel the rope got stuck. This meant that Adrian had to use the last of the twilight to climb up, free the rope, and rappel down again to the rest of the group before our final rappel in the dark onto the top of the U Notch. We needed to use headlamps for the rest of the descent. Down climbing the U-Notch seemed to take forever and was made more difficult for Deb by the discovery that she had lost her ice axe somewhere while rappelling off Polemonium. The icy section with fast flowing melt water was a small challenge and the bergschrund from above was a little tricky to find a route around. But, as Deborah discovered, Adrian was able to doze off while at a belay anchor and so he felt rested enough to figure out a way around it. Unfortunately, while Adrian was dozing he left behind one of our radios, and Ray later admitted to losing one as well, so we were down to only two. –

Adrian leads on Polmonium.

It was a tediously long slow descent by headlamp across the Palisade glacier, since the uneven surface of the "sun-cupped" hard snow was exceptionally difficult to walk on without twisting an ankle. Since we were all more than exhausted and it was well after midnight, we decided to try to bivvy for the night at the first quasi-level rock patch we could find. For shelter we had one nylon "bothy," a minimalist shelter, in which we could all crouch. The way it works is you put the bothy over your heads with everyone standing in a corner of the bothy. Then you all sit down at once with your knees up and your head resting on your knees. Everyone's legs were cramping and the ground was hard and stony. Although we tried to rest for an hour, and tried several different configurations with the bothy, we decided it would be better to keep moving, as we were all uncomfortable and cold.

Fatigue took its toll, as we made slow progress across the boulders and missed our trail. Suddenly, everything looked a lot less familiar, and we realized we were lost. We figured we would be able to navigate our way back a whole lot more accurately in daylight, so once again we decided to attempt using the bothy, this time on a rock above a shallow pool at 4:00 am, figuring a halt until the sun rose would do us no harm. We rested horizontally for an hour and a half, and managed to fall asleep for short bits until we would wake up shivering. Doze, freeze, slide into the water pool, shimmy back up, doze, freeze! We warmed up quickly once we began moving again at first light. We climbed up and over a gravel ridge to find the trail in the next valley. After 27 hours of climbing, we stumbled back into base camp, like zombies, at 7:00 am on Friday.

After dragging ourselves into camp, we quickly took care of the few necessary obligations we had, like filtering water and eating before collapsing into the tent for much needed sleep. We actually rested off and on the entire day, moving as little as possible, reading ahead about Thunderbolt and Starlight, doing crossword puzzles and Sudoku. We counted our losses: one crampon (Ray), two radios (Adrian and Ray), one ice axe (Deb), and a broken pole (Ryan). We wondered how these losses would affect us on our attempt on Starlight the next day. Deborah, who had a lot of problems with bad blisters on previous trips, was doing well in her new alpine boots. Thankfully, no one had suffered from altitude sickness, not even a headache. On our previous trip we had discovered the joys of "Cowboy Coffee," which is delicious "pour over" type coffee filtered through a bandana, and we drank it down in buckets on Friday. The weather was mostly cool with a light sprinkling of rain off and on all day; perfect for a rest day.

We awoke Saturday at 3:00 am to start our second summit day, and as hard as we had tried the night before to prepare so we could be off in half an hour, we still did not leave until nearly 4:00 am. Ryan took over as enthusiastic "alpha dog," leading our route, and this time Ryan, Adrian, Ray, and even Deb were careful to pay attention to where our return route would be.

Deborah rappels through the 'rabbit hole'.

It looked to be a fine day weather-wise. The route leading to the summit ridge was a little easier because the boulders we needed to cross were on the ridge and less likely to be unstable and wobbly. We took the Underhill Couloirs Route towards Starlight, and, being the youngest and decidedly strongest, Ryan was unanimously elected to be the one to kick steps in the snow for the rest of us to follow—exhausting work. Fortunately for all, the snow was of excellent quality, and Deborah was just fine using a ski pole instead of an ice axe, while 'Hopalong' Ray managed well with just one crampon. Once we left the snow we took Class 3 boulders up to the arête where some tricky exposed moves, led by Ryan, got us to the main ridge of Thunderbolt and Starlight at 10:30 am. For Deborah, this climb was ridiculously scary, and she had to remain incredibly focused to maintain her composure, since on numerous occasions she was maneuvering above fantastic thousand-foot drop-offs around every boulder.

We inched toward the summit of Starlight with Ryan still in the lead with incredible exposure and views. By this point Deborah had moved into the second tie-in position behind Ryan, which is actually the most secure position, so it greatly reduced her fears on exposed rock, and kept everyone moving along much faster. To keep from freaking out on the rocks with such steep exposure, Deborah made it a point to look straight ahead of her next move, trust the ropes, and, as much as possible, to not look down. She also tried to remain composed, even though internally she was an anxious mess. Ryan, for his part, was a fabulous "Horse Whisperer," frequently making reassuring comments such as, "I'm anchored solid," "You are going nowhere if you slip," "This is super easy, Deborah. You can totally do this." We came to a position about 200 feet from the summit, able to look back over the top of Thunderbolt at 14,003 feet elevation. Here we had to climb around the pinnacles of the ridge, airy flutes of rock with sheer sides. Ryan took a look at the blank wall ahead of him, and discussed a turnaround time of 3:30 pm. For the first time Deborah saw signs of uncertainty on his face. He made a valiant attempt at a dicey traverse, only to find more smooth wall ahead. Adrian took a second look and confirmed that we were over our heads with this route, only 200 vertical feet from the summit. The alternative route appeared to be hours away, down and around to the next gully. It was finally decided that since we would need to return for Thunderbolt anyway, we might as well plan for a return using a west side route that appeared a little easier for both Thunderbolt and Starlight.

We took several rappels down, this time being very careful to avoid a stuck rope. The second rappel was a fantastic descent through a hole in a jumble of crazily precarious rocks. From this vantage point at the top of the rappel we saw two climbers on the summit of Thunderbolt debating with each other about the best way down. Another rappel got us back down to the Underhill Couloir where we regrouped. We were relieved to be off the precarious ridges before dark, and vowed to get more "Beta" before attempting Starlight again. We again rappelled some low-angle snow and slipped and slid down to the relative safety of the Palisade glacier. Although we rarely saw many people on our climbs, as we crossed the glacier we met a young solo climber who was attempting to complete climbing all of the 14ers in the lower 48 states and was climbing Thunderbolt, Starlight, and Muir in the next 3 days. Despite the fact that we were disappointed at our lack of success that day, we wished him good luck. We hiked back into camp just before twilight, without the navigational issues of the day before, having completed a 17-hour day.

We were pleased to have achieved the two summits that we did reach, and this trip reiterated the difficulty of finding the best route. We decided we would do a little research before our return next year, and try a different route on the west side, in conjunction with an attempt at Thunderbolt Peak.

Split Mountain.

Chapter 7
SPLIT MOUNTAIN IN WINTER

14,065 feet
Summary: Winter Attempt of Split Mountain. Tough, tough and tougher... Also known as "The snow is too deep, the hill is too steep and the wind is too strong."
January 14th - 17th, 2010
Our Team: Adrian Crane, Deborah Steinberg, Carey Gregg, Derek Castle, Ryan Swehla.

We knew from the start that success during a winter ascent of any snow-covered mountain depended on "Good Roads, Good Snow, and Good Weather," and so before departing we asked the cyber-community to pray for synchronicity on our behalf.

This was going to be our first official 14er without Ray, who was scheduled for knee surgery the next morning. We left Modesto Wednesday evening with our bundles of packs, snowshoes, ski poles and other gear stuffed into the bed of Adrian's son's dual cab truck. Adrian warned us that the only problem with taking Jonathan's truck was that it didn't start well in cold weather. Hmmm...Ados, you know this is January, right? As Deborah's legs were shortest, she was relegated to the middle of the back seat with her legs squished into the middle console. Searching for a roadside place to camp, at 2am Thursday morning we pulled over and slept under the stars at the former site of the Post Office of Manzanar Internment Camp where, shamefully, 10,000 Japanese-Americans were held during the Second World War. It was a chilly night, and the ghosts of Manzanar haunted our sleep.

We woke up at 7 am, still groggy from our late arrival. We were in need of breakfast, and having been told the breakfast burritos at the Chevron in Big Pine were the best around we made a stop there. Knowing full well we were going to live on dehydrated food for the next few days, we pigged out on the best gas station food any of us had ever eaten. We then left the main highway and made the 12-mile drive over snowy dirt roads to find the Red Mountain Creek trailhead. The herds of deer along the track were the largest we had ever seen, although they were obviously perplexed at why humans would be crazy enough to be going into the wild in these winter conditions. The roads treated us well.

Carey snowshoes toward Split Mountain.

Before we left, we had heard about the possibility of a storm arriving

Sunday, and made an initial plan to attempt to hike all the way in to a single base camp Thursday, summit Friday, and return Saturday before the arrival of the storm. We had also been told there was a 20% chance of snow on Saturday.

Since we had dawdled over everything, from which food and gear to leave behind to Adrian's still unpacked backpack, we did not start out on the trail until noon. It was an exceptionally steep start. We managed to find the trail in patchy snow but then lost it again. Initially, we saw the tracks of many deer and rabbits, and in at least one case the tracks of a mountain lion. Snow cover increased to the point where we sunk knee deep, necessitating us to break out the snowshoes. We slipped and struggled through deep fluffy fresh powder on steep hillsides, and our ski poles were useless as they sunk all the way down to the hilt. The snow was often blanketing thick brush which only increased the instability. Deborah cursed a black streak as we went through a particularly tough stretch. Derek needed therapy after listening to how much she was struggling with her heavy backpack and the simple snow shoes that were not adequate for this type of terrain. Our mood was lightened only by Ryan's encouragement that he would take us to the nearby hot springs if we got out on Saturday.

The unforgiving slickness of the powdery snow and the steepness of our trail made our progress so slow that at 4:30 pm we realized we were far from reaching our goal of camping at Red Lake, and even farther from any good camping areas. In every direction we had only steep snowy slopes with rock or brush poking through. Since we had made little progress and still overlooked the Owens valley, we still had cell reception. A text message from Ray came in saying that the Sierras were expecting 10 feet of snow on Sunday night. Knowing Ray's tendency towards misspelled words and typos, Adrian declared that this was impossible and he must have meant 10 inches, unless it was a joke. Later another message came in to confirm it was indeed 10 feet. Was this the storm of the century coming in? The possibility of the storm arriving early never left Deborah's mind, and she worried about the already difficult conditions. It was scheduled to arrive by Sunday evening, but we knew that with the fickleness of weather forecasting it could easily hit us a few hours early. It was not only that we might be struggling back through deep fresh snow but once at the trailhead we might find ourselves snowed in and stranded 12 miles from the nearest real road. We discussed our options and decided to press on for the moment. We climbed higher to check the base of the cliffs above and found a site with minimal sloping which we managed to level by filling in with brush and snow to form an airy platform for our tent. Ryan and Carey's natural ingenuity came in handy as they expertly used snow stakes and Derek's snowshoes to make a structural framework for the branches and snow infill. We shoved five slightly stinky climbers into the four-person tent. Although exhausted and frustrated at our lack of progress, we slept amazingly well and warm, tight as matches in a box. Good snow conditions were not to be in the stars for us on this trip.

We were up at 7am with the sun. We experienced arduous hiking and snowshoeing all day with sections of snowy rock and deep powder on consistently steep landscape. The rough steep terrain had us slipping and tripping over and over again, and every misstep was rewarded with a heavy pack pinning us to the ground, requiring utmost efforts to heave back up again. We finally reached the unnamed small lake below Red Lake at 10,200 feet by 3:30pm. We decided to camp there as our progress in the soft snow with heavy backpacks was particularly grueling, and we would cover the ground far faster with just summit packs the next morning. Ryan and Adrian suggested different campsites each claiming theirs to be most superior and sheltered. We chose Ryan's windy site over Adrian's extremely windy one! As the tent was pitched, Deb mistakenly stepped around the tent without snowshoes and sunk into the soft snow, creating a hole outside the tent door. Attempting to turn this accident into a positive camp asset, she declared we should have a foot well outside the tent door. Derek was the unlucky one pressed into manual service to dig out the rest of the hole while Deb watched. She would have leaned on a shovel, supervisor-style, but we only had the one! With the tent up, we pumped water from a small open patch in the lake, cooked our dehydrated meals, made a fire, dried boots and socks and crawled into the still cramped tent at 7:50pm. Derek slept with his wet boots inside his sleeping bag in an attempt to dry them before morning while Deborah took a late night outing to shovel snow on the fire as the wind was whipping sparks from the not quite dormant fire in the direction of the tent.

Having discussed the pending mega-storm, we decided to make our summit attempt as early as possible so we would then have a chance to make our getaway as swift as was feasible on Sunday. We set two watches to a 2:00 am alarm even as we swore we would never hear them. Possibly because of anxiety about our summit attempt the next morning, most of us slept fitfully, and someone was always awake either because of an elbow in the side when someone rolled over or the freight train noise as the wind gusts hurtled through the trees and then whipped at the fabric. Thus, the alarms were heard! It was the always-cheerful Derek who roused himself first, much like an enthusiastic Thumper to his unenthusiastic tent-mates, bubbling encouraging words, while the rest of us responded with grunts and half-closed eyes. Derek, a former pastor-turned-construction worker is the most upbeat person on this planet. It could be bitter cold and windy outside, and he would stick his head out the tent, and say in his Australian accent, "Ahhh... isn't it beautiful here, Dehbrah?" Derek also loves to learn new languages, so often Deborah and Derek would pass time on a long section of trail by practicing conversational Spanish with each other.

A bitter cold wind kept blowing out the fragile flames of our camp stove.

After struggling for half an hour, we dove back in the tent with the two stoves in the vestibule and made breakfast inside in a jumble of down sleeping bags, hissing stoves, and precariously balanced cups of tea and hot chocolate. Powder snow floated in through the vents.

We had a serious discussion about the wisdom of trying for the summit in this weather. Derek was the voice of reason – he went out to get ready!

We left camp at 3:45 am, carrying our memento of 2-year-old Chase Shlenker, reminding ourselves that our misery was not ours alone. We set off up the valley on snowshoes in pitch black with the wind booming around us. No moon, few stars, and no pre-dawn light offered no respite from the darkness. We navigated by compass, and amazingly hit Red Lake where we filled water bottles from a slush on top of the lake ice.

Above the lake, we climbed on snowshoes up the snow-covered moraines toward the false summit. At 11,300 feet, about halfway up, the faint light of dawn permitted us to make out the bulk of Split above us to the left and the false summit ahead of us to the North West. The wind now blew even harder with frequent strong gusts and little mercy. We all felt the cold from the incessant wind. Adrian had to put on a down jacket, the first time he had found that necessary in the Sierras while climbing. Ryan and Deborah's feet were both suffering from the beginnings of frostbite, and Carey, always the first to be affected by altitude, wasn't feeling too exuberant. Amazingly, Derek's enthusiasm from first hearing the watch at 2:00 am never waned, and he led through the snow, occasionally pulling out his video camera to shoot a short vignette. As we approached the false summit at 12,000 feet, dawn had indeed arrived, but the wind was escalating, and gusts would threaten to knock us over. We had to pause and brace ourselves, hiding our faces and eyes from the stinging snow crystals. Derek and Adrian had anticipated that the wind would dissipate after dawn, but we had no such luck. The sky was dark with what looked like an impending storm, and there was no warmth from the little sunlight we had. We looked across at the chute that led to the Sierra crest which would be a long exhausting climb in deep powder. If the wind was this bad here we could only guess how bad it was on the crest. Derek shot a video of the howling wind and driven snow just to prove our predicament!

In the face of the brutal wind and already suffering the effects of the cold that it caused us, we agreed to turn around. It was 7:45 am and we had made it to 12,000 feet. Because we were carrying only our light summit packs, we actually made much better progress on this day even while the snow conditions remained less than ideal. However, wind and cold had the upper hand, and we retreated knowing we had pushed as far as we could. On the way down, the winds continued to increase, and we endured several gusts where blowing spindrift engulfed us in a whiteout. We guessed wind speeds of 60 miles an hour. Deborah's knee finally succumbed to the efforts of the last two and a half days and she tweaked it during another slip, it having been hammered just one time too many. She trod very delicately from there on.

The upper slopes of Split Mountain in gale force winds.

We were back in camp by 9:20 am and agreed to continue the trek out after we had eaten and packed up camp. Hot springs here we come – or maybe a motel with a hot tub. Before the tent was taken down, Adrian indulged in a 15 minute nap which improved his demeanor considerably.

The trip out was quicker and easier than the hike in as we were going steeply downhill, but sheer slopes still made for technical snowshoeing with plenty of slips and falls, slides and stumbles. Snowshoes disappeared in deep holes beside rocks. Derek found unexpected obstacles as he led and ended up headfirst buried under the snow. He was still smiling as Ryan gave him a hand up. Several short glissades aided our progress, the best being a several-hundred foot slide ending with a 6 foot drop over a little rock pile. Ryan and Deborah had simple snowshoes not well suited to steep going, and Deborah's knee got worse with every slip. We managed to follow our own trail and retrace the route for the most part even though it had been filled in by blowing snow. At one point, Derek took a shortcut, but the snow was so deep and powdery he couldn't snowshoe out. He extricated himself by using the branches of small trees that were mostly buried under the snow, pulling himself from one tree to the next. Adrian came around a corner to find both Ryan and Derek head-first down a fresh chute of snow. Ryan popped his head up smiling and commented how it was "an intentional maneuver". Tripping on buried brush, Deborah added a head-over-heels to her repertoire of snowshoe moves.

At 2:00 pm, the sun dropped behind the high ridges to the south of our canyon and we were plunged into chilly temperatures, warm enough when moving but instantly chilling as soon as we stopped; especially if that stop involved the immersion of our body in powder snow.

At dusk, after 14 hours of hiking and 16 hours after waking, we emerged from the canyon and could look down on the truck at the trailhead below.

Our prayers were answered as the truck started with barely a stammer despite the cold. We had a 45 minute drive out on the dirt road. We were tremendously grateful we had not been pinned down by the approaching storm. Looking back at the Sierras, the high peaks were clear and the storm had clearly not hit. Was there a twinge of regret on Adrian's face?

We went to a rustic café in Big Pine where our 6:30 pm arrival just beat the closing time of 7:00 pm, which we thought rather early for a Saturday night in a hopping place like this. We deduced that we either smelled really bad or that the waitress had a favorite TV show at 7:30 and desperately wanted to be home by then as she appeared somewhat reluctant to serve us. Fish of the day? "Sorry we're out." I'll have the soup. "Sorry, out of soup, but I can do a salad." How about a slice of one of your three varieties of homemade pie? "Can't get you the pie." May I have more water for my tea? "Well, I'll try." "A refill of coffee?" "You mean you want me to make a fresh pot just for you?" At this point Deborah returned from ten minutes in the restroom, having done the best to clean up her body and fingernails with wet wipes and was finally able to order. Adrian had not enamored himself to the staff as he left the restroom key locked in the restroom which resulted in a head in hands moment for the waitress.

With new snow still predicted for the Sierras, we decided to return home by the southern route rather than over the high passes to the North which could be slow going or closed altogether. Afraid that Adrian would insist that we camp out another night, Ryan used his fancy smartphone and Adrian's long ago memories of Lone Pine to find a motel which had a hot tub. We happily drove by the parking lot at Manzanar, where we had rough-camped on the trip in, and this time enjoyed the relative luxury of the Dow Villa and a room with 3 beds split between five. As Deborah had her own cot, the guys decided it was okay to share a bed as long as one guy would sleep under the sheet, and the other would sleep over the sheet. We fulfilled our need for a warm reward by enjoying the hot tub, submerged to the chin in hot water while the frigid January air threatened to freeze our eyebrows.

Sunday morning's breakfast at the Alabama Hill Café more than made up for the debacle at the diner in Big Pine, and the only hiccup occurred when Derek's Spanish wasn't good enough to understand the waitress' offer of 'jello' squash' meant 'yellow squash'. We even took the time to play tourist on this trip. We allowed ourselves an hour to drive around the Alabama Hills area where many of the movies from the 1940's and '50's were made. We followed the road tour, looking at the piles of boulders which formed shapes such as "the elephant," "the cougar," and "the football player" - figures easy to imagine with lingering high altitude delirium.

As we gently toured these natural sculptures, we reminisced about our adventure, the weather, the snow conditions and Deborah's knee. Had we made the right decision to turn around? It was noon and the feared storm had still not arrived.

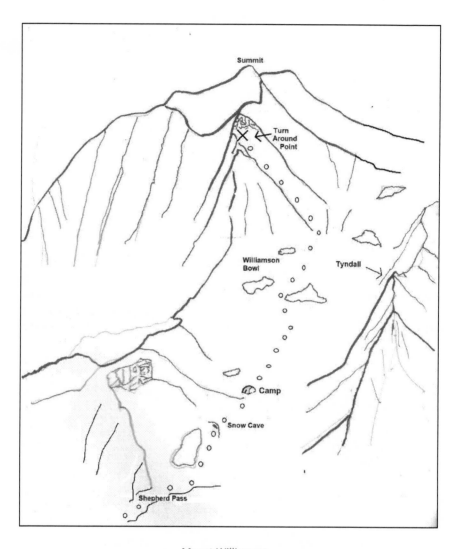

Mount Williamson.

Chapter 8
WILLIAMSON AND TYNDALL

May 12th- 16th 2010
Summary: Oh so close on Williamson, but we did make Tyndall.
Also known as "Eeeny, meeny, miney, moe, which gully shall we go....."
Our Team: Adrian Crane, Deborah Steinberg, Ray Kablanow, Carey Gregg.

After the near disastrous trail and snow conditions during our January attempt of Split Mountain, Deborah had much to panic about after learning that the approach to base camp for this climb was going to be our longest ever -- about 12 miles and 6000 vertical feet in elevation gain. Actually, it was nearly 7000 total feet vertical gain if you include the big drop in elevation the trail makes in the middle of the trip.

Adrian decided to bring along a 'travois', otherwise known as a "wheelshaw," a device designed for transporting a deer carcass through the woods, to move heavier group gear, such as the tent, snowshoes, and ice axes, as far as it would go. We all vowed to go as light as possible as we were expecting a much less technical climb of both mountains, and were able to leave behind a lot of heavier gear. Ounce by ounce we shaved weight off our packs by bringing fewer clothes, and nothing that was not absolutely essential. So, with a sawed-off toothbrush and 5 days' worth of sunblock re-packed into an artificial tears bottle, we set off on Wednesday morning. Since we dawdled endlessly at the trailhead on our last climb, Deborah was pleased that we left at a relatively early start of 9:00 am on the well-marked trail.

We soon discovered the reason the trip to base camp was going to be so long was because of the endless switchbacks up and down the mountainside. On the east side of the mountain, the wheelshaw struggled through piles of detritus leftover from a rock slide, many stream crossings, and the frequent patches of snow that often obscured the trail. The joke was that Adrian would hand over the travois to Carey whenever a major obstacle was imminent. Frequently, it took one to pull and a second to navigate and assist through the obstacles. Whether the overall effect of having the travois was actually beneficial was hotly debated. We camped the first night at Mahogany Flat at about 8500 feet, where we found a pleasant campsite by the stream with a nearby tree ideal for hanging our food. Although bear canisters are way more convenient, they are also heavy, and we knew we would be camping low enough to be bothered by bears only on the first night. Thus, in our desire to be efficient and lightweight, the canisters were left behind and we spent a good 20 minutes fiddling to get the rope over a solid branch. By the time we left Mahogany Flat the next morning, we had at last decided to ditch both our snowshoes and the ungainly travois device.

Ray, Adrian and Carey on Shepherd Pass

Although we had a long way to go, the trail was good for the next 7 miles, and we had time to enjoy stories and conversation to keep ourselves moving along. Occasionally, Deborah would relay college stories from when she was a bona fide sorority girl in Sigma Kappa at UCLA. During Sorority Recruitment, also known as "Sorority Rush," being polite was always the rule, no matter how awkward or odd the conversation turned. It is no wonder that sorority girls do well in job interviews, because they have had so much practice being outstanding conversationalists that they could literally talk to a wall, or at least a very shy collegiate. During one rush party, one of Deborah's sorority sisters was paired with a young collegiate who wore a large brightly colored green and red jacket and large dark sunglasses that she wore during the entire Rush Party. She kept mentioning how she loved visiting "Frahhnce" and that her boyfriend was from "Frahhnce," and she would make large sweeping motions with her hands. Deborah's friend thought maybe she was being punked, and that this whole conversation was going to end up on television, because this quirky girl was not like your average Freshman collegiate, let alone someone interested in joining a sorority, but it definitely made the conversation memorable.

After many more stories and discussions, we reached the beginning of Shepherd Pass where it was time to strap on crampons and really begin climbing. At this point, Deborah was nervous about how her right knee, injured during the winter Split Mountain trip, was going to hold up and wore a neoprene knee brace. Ray, recently recovered from knee surgery, wore a complimentary high-tech brace on his left knee. There were many areas where sinking through the snow into a post hole was an issue, and the two travelled through these places with great caution.

Finally, we roped up and slogged our way up Shepherd Pass together, each with their own mantra: "One step, two step, three step rest. One step, two step, three step, rest..... "Occasionally would come the call of "Break!", and we would all stop for 30 seconds before continuing on. The prize at the top of the pass was a breathtaking view into Sequoia National Park of snow-covered mountains with frequently changing fog and cloud patterns to the west, and a brilliant natural ice cave to the south.

Although we were exhausted and it was a little out of the way, we decided to investigate the ice cave. A snow hare scampered across our path, wondering what we were doing there. There were curves and ribbons of ice in every direction in the massive house-sized cave. Although it was deep, no one had the nerve to explore too extensively. Adrian tried to torment Deborah by poking at the ceiling with his ski pole, proclaiming, "See, this is solid!" which Deborah knew better than to trust.

Shortly after this diversion, it started to snow, and we began in earnest to decide where to camp. We were now at 12,000 feet and Carey was dragging from the altitude. We set up camp on the southeast side of a little bowl at about 4:00 pm where we had plenty of rocks to help serve as "kitchen." From here, our open view of the ever-changing weather decorating the mountains was most spectacular. Deborah declared this her favorite camp site. We did not have to spend too much time getting ready for our summit attempt the next day since most of the gear that was not for sleeping or cooking had to be brought with us anyhow. Although we were all a little spent, we managed to choke down hot noodle soup and our freeze-dried dinners before stumbling into the tent at about 7:00 pm.

Ray, Deborah and Adrian at the ice cave.

By now the snow was falling steadily, and Deborah started to have anxiety about how much snow would be too much. The guys were none too stressed, since only an inch of snow had been forecast. A small flask of some type of alcoholic beverage was passed around, and Deborah relaxed slightly about the weather. Since it was fairly early and way too cold to hang outside the tent, we did a group attempt at a crossword puzzle, and we found that Sudoku at 12,500 feet is not as easy as at lower altitudes. All but Ray had a headache, and we could already tell that Carey was not going to be fit to attempt Williamson with us the next morning. We started to doubt the wisdom of camping so high. However, sometimes it can be quite entertaining as we often share ridiculous stories, especially since the effects of even a little Bourbon at altitude is magnified. Deborah relayed the humorous tale of how one of her co-workers was accidentally named by the hospital. When she was born, her parents had decided to call her Lorena, but at the hospital her mother's handwriting was so poor, it was interpreted as "Linnsee". Her family noticed the error, and originally intended to keep calling her Lorena, but every time her grandmother said her name with her heavy accent it sounded like she was saying "diarrhea" so eventually the family decided "Linnsee" was a fine name.

Waking at 6:05 am, Deborah gave the "15 more minutes" order, so we all gladly slept in a little before rousing in the thin air. No one was exceptionally keen about removing themselves from the tent, but we reminded ourselves that since we did not have Derek to encourage us to get moving we had to do it ourselves. We managed to set off at about 7:40 am for an attempt on Williamson. Our approach from this point was only a couple miles with one notable very long downhill section. Ray and Adrian remarked how much fun that was going to be to ascend on our return after a long day. As we looked at the west face of Williamson with its many chutes and spires, we consulted the guidebook to help us determine our direction. Most guidebooks are notoriously vague, but this book did specifically mention a dark band and watermark to help us determine the proper chute to ascend. Unfortunately, all these markers were covered in snow. Nevertheless, the guys felt confident, and we proceeded up a steep snow gully. At this point we were making pretty good progress and felt confident we would make the summit by 2 pm.

Adrian in the tent at our camp on Shepherd Pass

At the top of the chute all who watched us linger on SPOT in this location, probably wondered what we were doing. Still confident we were in the correct chute, we were looking for a small chasm to pass through the rocks with Class 3 scrambling to our right.

But there were a bunch of confusing choices of possible steep routes.

Maybe Williamson was not going to be as easy as we thought it should be. We tried the most likely looking route and Ray finally hauled himself up a 20 foot rock step. He threw the rope down, but Deb, in crampons and gloves, couldn't quite get up the section she was attempting, and swung gallantly on the rope several times before she decided to give up. Luckily Adrian did not need to attempt that particular pitch! Ray climbed up and round as Deb and Adrian made their way back over steep snow to the original gully. Ray threw a rope down a short pitch and we easily climbed up to join him. We continued up this gully to the top of the chute where, sure enough, there was a notch with views to the Owens Valley on the left and a Class 3 cleft on the right that we could easily scramble up. "Such relief, we are on route and should be to the summit soon," Adrian thought, but just around the corner we were stymied again. Teetering on steep icy snow and rock we attacked another questionable short Class 4 pitch, and Ray surmounted it again while Deb and Adrian followed. At the top, we found a sheer drop greeted us on the other side of a knife edge ridge and our progress right and left was blocked by cliffs. It was 4:35, half an hour past our 4:00 pm turn-around time. We were skunked again!!

Disappointed, we made our way down the mountain physically and emotionally spent after investing so much effort into attempting the summit. Ray had to downclimb a nasty step with only a minimal belay from Adrian that used every inch of rope and sling that we had. We reached the bottom of the snow gully at dusk. We were zombies as we struggled up the final hill into camp at 9:40 pm, but the good news was that Carey had hot water and food ready in a few minutes and we were happy to eat and drink before falling exhausted into the tent. We were so tired that we ate very little, even though we hadn't eaten much that day. Although enormously disappointed, we decided tomorrow we would take on Tyndall with a fresh attitude.

We managed to sleep in until almost 7:00 am the next morning, and we decided to take a rather steep shortcut to our intended route up Tyndall. We slogged uphill on the snow and ice until we eventually reached the rocky ridge. Deborah insisted on being roped up as we picked our way across the knife edge summit ridge for about a mile.

We came to a point where Deborah was worried that something would come up to skunk us for a fourth summit attempt in a row, but Ray put it all into perspective: "This is what you are climbing for! Cancer patients have challenges on a daily basis and at times can go into remissions. Likewise, people who are developmentally disabled have ongoing challenges and disappointments and times when they can't do what they would like to be doing." With a fresh appreciation for our task, we slowly picked our way across the ridge.

Although there was a fair amount of exposure on both sides of the ridge, there were good handholds and footholds that made it fairly easy once we

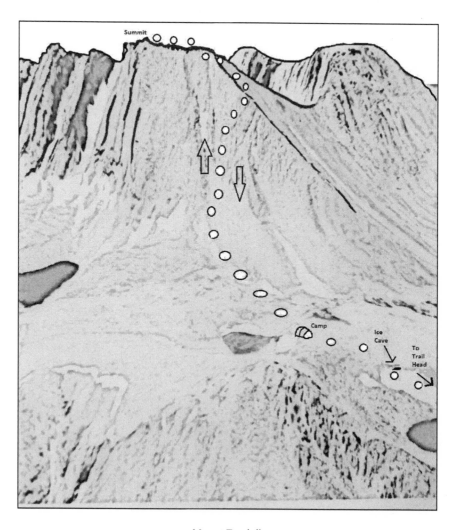

Mount Tyndall

got over the views of sharp drop-offs on the left and right. Finally, we
crested the summit of Mt. Tyndall! Deborah was feeling extra emotional as
we placed all the mementos into the summit box: a picture of a green rose
for her mother Rose Green who was recently diagnosed with Merkel cell
carcinoma, an angel pin for her friend Bart's mom, Nora Elizabeth Campbell,
who passed away from colon cancer in 2004, a photo of Chase Ryan
Schlenker, who was the young grandson of Anita Schlenker of Shadowchase
Running Club, and another medallion from Kristen Machado, who had her
arm amputated the week prior. After three failed summit attempts in a row,

it felt encouraging to finally have success. Carey radioed us at the summit saying that he could see us from camp and attempted to take a picture of what probably looked like black spots on the summit.

As we were descending, we ran into a young solitary Russian climber, who was so fast he made it up to the summit and back down before we made it all the way back to our camp! It was a humbling experience for our old bodies to see youth pass us by so quickly. Deborah reminded the guys that they should be glad they had her along as an "excuse" to explain why we moved so slowly. We were able to slide down some areas of snow, making Deborah very nervous she would lose control and wipe out, whereas Adrian and Ray were comfortable with sliding almost as fast as they could go. Carey was waiting for us with a hot dinner when we returned at 4:00 pm, and we prepared our gear for the next morning's long haul out. We wrote our field notes in the tent and tried to go to sleep early, but ended up chatting in the tent until about 9:00 pm. During our occasional forays outside at night, the Milky Way exploded in the sky and the mountains were still visible because of the reflection off the snow. We were prepared to return to civilization, but not yet ready.

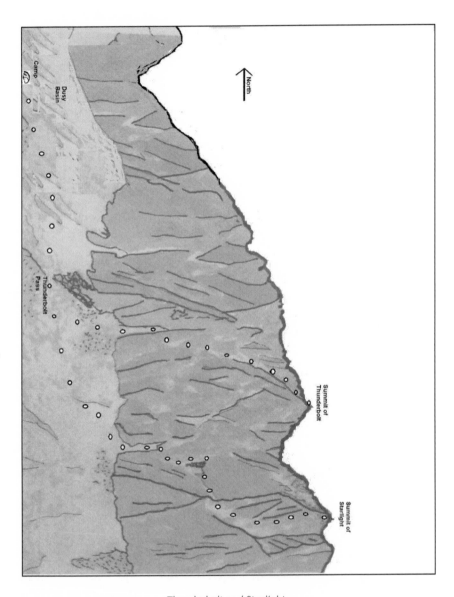

Thunderbolt and Starlight.

Chapter 9
THUNDERBOLT AND STARLIGHT

14,003 feet (Thunderbolt Peak) and 14,200 feet (Starlight) summits
July 7th - 11th
Also known as: "I can't believe we did that...."
Our Team: Adrian Crane, Deborah Steinberg, Ryan Swehla and Carey Gregg.

The challenges we face on every mountain include technical climbing, navigation, and endurance. This trip to Thunderbolt and Starlight had been our most anticipated trip, requiring the highest level of skill in many areas. Last year we hired a guide for a weekend training to work with us on our technical rock climbing and alpine mountaineering skills specifically for four peaks in the Palisades; North Palisade, Polemonium, Thunderbolt, and Starlight. With the help of Dave Miller, we gained skills that allowed us to succeed on the summits of North Pal and Polemonium, yet we had failed on our first attempt of Starlight and had yet to try Thunderbolt. We also had notably failed at navigation more than once, so we never felt confident that conditions alone would always allow a summit. With all this in mind, we vowed to bring along more trip reports collected from the internet along with the 14er guidebook to bolster our chances on these two notoriously difficult mountains. Our group was composed of the usual suspects: Adrian Crane, Deborah Steinberg, Ryan Swehla, and Carey Gregg. Notably absent from our regular group was Ray Kablanow, who was injured during a climbing accident while training a month prior and not well enough recovered to climb these mountains yet. Ray's accidental fall and failure of his pro-gear placement reminded us of the seriousness of our venture.

It was Wednesday morning when we left the South Lake trailhead (elevation 9,700 feet) at 10:30 am near Bishop, CA with one bear canister (to stay legal) and a permit. Deborah wore knee braces on both knees and donned a lighter pack than usual, thanks to the guys.

After a couple of hours, Deb declared herself out of fuel and in dire need of something substantial to eat! Ryan kept dangling the "around the next corner" carrot, but Deborah knew her body too well and stopped long enough to scoop out a large spoonful of peanut butter straight out of the jar and then continued moving. From then on, Deborah tried to stuff her pockets with plenty of high protein bars and became known as "the bartender." We finally moved out of the mosquito zone and stopped for a pleasant lunch of cheese, crackers, and dehydrated fruit.

Adrian, Carey and Deborah head into the gully toward Thunderbolt.

We headed up towards Bishop Pass on a good trail with little snow, passing many beautiful lakes and a few hikers. We saw the NFS Trail crew at work on an alternate trail, but once over the pass we saw no one for the rest of our time there. Once over Bishop Pass, we had to leave our nice little trail and head into Dusy Basin, hiking cross-country on rocky rolling terrain, patchy with snow fields. We set up camp at 5:15 pm at a pleasant but damp location near several large rocks. We were all tired on arrival but pleased to find a good campsite in the shelter of a huge boulder. Snow fields lapped at our camp area, but there was enough clear ground to pitch the tent and set up a kitchen area. We noted that we were all probably dehydrated.

We tried to get to bed quickly as we knew we had to be up early for the attempt on Thunderbolt. Deb and Carey slept on thick mattresses while Ryan and Ados got the deep, dark, cold, damp troughs between. To assist our bodies into slumber, Ryan passed a flask of bourbon. Deborah fell asleep before Adrian finished reciting the first of many poems about being in the snowy woods.

Ryan peeking around the summit block of Thunderbolt.

On Thursday, we woke as agreed at 5:00 am, but Deb immediately requested a 5 minute respite which we all enjoyed. We were vertical at 5:10, and breakfast was a quick process thanks to the bounty of wet water. We didn't need to melt snow and didn't even bother to filter. We left at 6:30 am, traversing over icy sun-cupped snow to Thunderbolt Pass with Ryan leading a circuitous route that involved as little altitude loss as possible. Adrian complained about the route. We left our hiking poles just over Thunderbolt pass at the base of the first chute. Because we had picked the wrong chute to ascend up Williamson during our last attempt, Deb made us confirm by checking multiple trip reports that we were indeed choosing the correct chute! At 8:00 am, we started up the chute on steep snow to the big chockstone that intercepted the route. According to more than one set of trip reports, we were to take a catwalk to the right which would lead to easier terrain. We were all a bit anxious that we might be defeated on our first peak of the trip, so we stuck to the directions in the trip report as closely as possible, which was something we had never before practiced. We found the shelf and edged across it.

We climbed higher and higher until the chute narrowed to a crawl under a large boulder which brought us out into a notch on the ridge. "Already here! Not bad so far," we agreed. It was 11am, and we were on the ridge. Ryan took a look at the class 5 pitch and declared "No worries." We followed Ryan's lead up the easy Class 5 pitch to a short Class 3 scramble and then to the final steep slabs across to the summit monolith. Carey wandered back and forth along the precariously exposed slabs while Deb, Adrian, and even Ryan beseeched him to be careful. It was noon when we assembled on the rocks at the eastern foot of the summit block.

The Summit block was 20 feet high, and exposed to thousand foot drops on three sides. The fourth side that faced us was smooth vertical granite with no obvious handholds. We prepared to throw a rope around the block but Ryan went ahead to check it out. Despite the terrifying exposure, he managed to work his way around on narrow ledges, and soon his voice began to echo back from the south rather than the north. Suddenly, we saw his head emerge on the south side! After attaching to a tenuous belay, he inched back to the west edge and hung. Adrian threw a cord attached to a rock-weighted bag over the top of the block, and lowered it to him. We pulled the climbing rope back over and belayed Ryan. Carey and Ryan then waited for each other's' verbal signal to start climbing, thinking the other would make the first call. After a couple of minutes of standoff, the miscommunication was sorted out and Ryan began climbing the west side. We heard a stream of grunting and expletives, but soon he was straddling the summit itself, and collapsed in a heap on top. He was exhilarated, yet completely exhausted from the most difficult Class 5 climbing he had ever attempted. Secretly Deborah, Carey and Adrian mumbled a little prayer of thanks that Ryan was along to solve the summit block issue. It was 1:00 pm. Ryan clipped another length of rope into a fixed anchor that happened to be at the top of the block and rappelled back to clear his protective gear and ropes. With the belay rope affixed to the summit, Carey climbed it in good style and touched the top at 1:40 pm. Deb and Adrian followed to take their turns touching the dramatically exposed precipice of the summit block. Deborah required a boost to start her unstylized shimmy up the smooth face, but managed to get her hand on the summit. Although we didn't all climb it completely unassisted, each of us touched the true summit with the help of our teammates, which is what climbing a mountain is all about.

We signed the log book and placed mementos in the summit box in memory of David Kitzmann who had lung cancer, and in honor of Rochelle Rosen who has colo-rectal cancer. Although we saw no one, we heard a human shout but couldn't quite locate it in the cliffs below; they were probably on North Palisade. Fortunately, the weather was warm and tranquil, so playing on the summit block for two hours was no problem. We were thrilled to have made it. Deb and Adrian admitted they were worried that this trip might be a complete bust, and indeed we were the first summiteers in 2 weeks. Carey has found altitude a huge problem on past climbs but was feeling good and climbing strongly so he had a big grin on his face. We cleared our gear and headed back.

Another rabbit hole under a boulder took us to the rappel. Carey did not have his rappel device so we lowered him down the class 5 pitch to the notch and then rappelled after him. In the notch, we had lunch and were amused by a Marmot who seemed to have no fear of us or of steep exposed rock. We descended the steep chute, careful not to dislodge rocks to the last rappel over the chockstone to the easy snow slope below that led to the Palisade basin. It had already been a lengthy but successful day. We knew that the next day we would come this way to Starlight so we left our climbing gear in a cache to save carrying it down to camp and then back up. It was 6:00 pm by the time we left Thunderbolt Pass and slowly staggered back onto the snow that had been warmed and softened by the day's sun. It was a slog from Thunderbolt Pass to camp. Deep post holes and the occasional melt-out near a rock ambushed our weary bodies. It would have been dreary except that we were still very excited about summiting what we knew to be a very difficult peak. Carey finally got sick from the altitude and Deborah asked him kindly if he could possibly barf out of earshot so that she would not gag as well. Deb had to take it slowly to save her knee, but we were lucky the weather was still perfect, lessening our worries that we would need to hurry back (not that we could speed up if we wanted to). We returned back to camp at 7:15 pm and shared a little bourbon to celebrate our success as we watched the sunset, enjoying the beautiful plays of light and peach-colored alpine glow on the granite peaks and icy lakes. There really was no time to spare, so we headed straight to bed after dinner in preparation for another early rise tomorrow for an attempt at Starlight.

First light on Friday broke at 5:00 am, and again we indulged in "just 5 more minutes." Suddenly, it was 5:30 and we tumbled out of the tent. Deb narrated a strange dream about chockstones and trip reports as we started to rouse. We prepared to leave after choking down another breakfast of oatmeal, after which everyone decided we were sick of oatmeal for breakfast, and vowed never to bring it on another trip. At least we had Starbucks Vias, which is pretty decent instant coffee for a wilderness trip. Carey decided to stay back as he never did eat dinner yesterday and prior to that had lost any lunch he might have had! We left camp at 6:40 am and made it to Thunderbolt Pass after an hour following another of Ryan's circuitous routes while Adrian again grumbled. This time we followed last night's tracks that cut through the soft snow, so it was easier going. We reached the gear cache and loaded up our packs with an excessive variety of pro-gear and ropes to give us the means to tackle any eventuality. At Deb's insistence, we re-read the trip notes and confirmed the correct chute to be the final one before the big west buttress; a large snow covered fan would be our best clue. It was 8:15 am. We climbed steep but easy snow to another chockstone blockage and then followed obvious ledges on the right as we gained height. We backtracked a few times as we followed the intricate route that maintained Class 3 difficulty. The terrain did get a little easier after a couple of hundred feet, and, using pictures in the trip notes that we had, we easily found the subsidiary chute that led up to snow-covered slabs. At the top of the slabs, we peeked out over the steep drop into the next chute. It looked fearsome, but, sure enough, the catwalk to the left was easy, although very exposed, and deposited us into the center of the chute. Not a fan of small catwalks, Deborah calmed herself a bit with the reminder that we were roped up, but still had to convince herself that everyone would not be pulled over the edge to their death if she slipped off the narrow traverse.

Ahead was the waterfall as mentioned in the notes. It was iced over and looked impossibly steep from our vantage point, but Ryan tackled it with his usual tenacity. After a few minutes and light showers of swear words, ice, and rocks tumbling down to us, he declared he was over the top and had a belay for us. Deb and then Adrian followed on the rope and made it into the steep chute above the waterfall. A little way up the chute, a large snowfield covered the center. Adrian took to the snow while Ryan and Deb skirted it and climbed bedrock ledges to the left. Halfway up the snow, Adrian decided it was quite steep and felt rather exposed out by himself. There was no choice for him, however, so he soldiered on, keeping pace with Ryan and Deb and joined them where the snow field dissipated. We were on a sharp incline of rubble-covered bedrock, and Deb and Adrian were nervous about the consistent exposure. Ryan, unphased, led confidently and unroped with encouraging words to both. Finally, Adrian and Deb persuaded Ryan that we would be happier with a rope and that maybe we would move faster that way, rather than slower. The chute steepened and spread into several possible routes. We checked the trip notes, but the route was not obvious, so we made our own way up Class 4 rock until Ryan yelled back that he had reached the ridge. Now where was that "milk bottle" shaped summit block?

Deborah and Adrian on the 'catwalk' to Starlight.

We began an airy scramble, but in just a few yards we glimpsed through a wide crack that the milk bottle was on the other side! It was easy to slide through the crevice, and we found ourselves sitting at the foot of the obelisk, the infamous "Milk Bottle." It looked a lot taller than we expected.

By then, it was 2:00 pm and sunny, but there was a chilling wind. Deb wrote in the register as Adrian and Ryan rigged the ropes. Steve Porcella, author of *Climbing California's Fourteeners* and a supporter of 'Climb for a Cure' had put this summit register in place, and coincidentally we were climbing now in honor of his mother Yvonne. We signed the log book also in honor of Sandra Enloe-Burger. We threw a rope across the east shoulder, and Ryan crawled up the south arête. Then, he threw a second cord around the west side and we pulled the climbing rope around after it. Ryan clipped in and was now belayed by a rope all around the spire and comfortable enough that he climbed to victory at 2:30 pm. He clipped the rope into the fixed bolt anchor at the top, backing it up with a new sling and rappelled off. We were pleasantly shocked by our second success. Now that the obelisk had been fixed with a top rope by Ryan, Deb was able to summit after some amazingly ungraceful moves, followed by Adrian. We radioed Carey that we were ecstatic over having this second difficult summit behind us. We were again the first summiteers in 2 weeks.

Behind the milk bottle and out of the wind, it was warmer, but steady cold gusts made it uncomfortable to be out of the sheltered spot. We pulled our gear, ate lunch hastily and left at 3:30 pm for the long descent. We had several interesting rappels, one ending on a 5-foot slab wedged halfway down a cliff, and each of us refrained from voicing our concerns over how well attached it might be. On one rap, we found 180 feet of existing double ropes and felt like we had scored a free descent. We retraced our route, moving short-roped and making slow but steady progress. As we approached the bottom we tried to get within our 60 foot rappel range of the chockstone and followed ledges down as they appeared. Just as we felt we were within range of the rappel we realized we could follow a last few ledges and zig zag to the snow in the floor of the chute. We put on our crampons and slipped and slid down the snow out of the confines of the chute into the late evening of Palisade basin. Finally, we were onto easy ground at 7:30 pm and picked up the remaining items from our cache just below Thunderbolt Pass shortly after. On the pass at 8:10 pm, we radioed Carey to put on the hot water. Our version of Queen's *Bohemian Rhapsody*; "Thunderbolt and Starlight, very very frightening ..." richoched though our heads. We were thrilled but tired. We unanimously declared that Ray would have to find himself another guide because none of us was ready to repeat Starlight! The snow was beginning to re-freeze as we descended Thunderbolt Pass to camp, so the conditions underfoot were not bad. Adrian retraced his route from the evening before, although it included a little up and down which Ryan good naturedly pointed out. As dusk descended, we hadn't quite made it back in the last light of the evening and moved by the light of headlamps. Our spirits rose as we were welcomed by Carey flashing his light from camp.

Adrian on the airy 'milkbottle' summit of Starlight.

The slight rise as we came into camp slowed our progress, but we were heartened by Carey's welcome, the promise of hot drinks, and the beckon of a hot meal. We celebrated again but were quickly persuaded into the tent by the arctic breeze.

After our unexpected success on consecutive days we still had a spare day available so Ryan expanded his horizons to include an attempt on Mount Sill the next day. Knowing that Adrian cannot resist a challenge, Ryan commented that he should come along '…unless you are too tired!' Carey also agreed to try Sill as he had had a rest day. Deb was only too happy to look after camp and enjoyed a rare day of quiet and self-indulgence having summited Sill in 2008. Ryan agreed an early start was not necessary. How long to Sill from here? Maybe 6 hours guessed Adrian – no, no, make that 10. We agreed maybe it wouldn't be such an easy day. And so we happily stumbled to bed.

It was 5:30 am on Saturday and everyone was awake. Deb once again narrated her latest dream of the Yeti and glissading off a cliff which made everyone doze in wonderful warmth till 6:30 am. Even though she was not coming with us, Deb got up to help boil water, cook breakfast (oatmeal. again!), and send everyone on their way. We left at 7:42 am with the sky heavy with ominous clouds. Since this was Ryan's trip, Adrian let him lead his contouring route to Thunderbolt Pass, but Adrian coined the term AltiVariPhobia (or as Deborah was to later call it "IsoAltiphilia") for the likes of Ryan who hates to gain or lose altitude. Ryan sunk into a deep hole camouflaged by snow, and we had to dig him free. Once over Thunderbolt Pass, there was a lot more of the rock and treacherous sun-cupped snow mixture in the miles around Palisade basin to Potluck Pass. We cut upwards before Potluck, skirted a snowfield, and ascended the rubble and boulders of Peak 13,900, the incorrectly named Polemonium peak on the topo map. We saw the clouds massing on the horizon as the weather shifted. Rain squalls were south of us. Adrian felt vulnerable as he had packed light for this day and had not expected bad weather. As luck would have it, he found a faded stuff sack with emergency gear and a space blanket in an old bivvy site and as he put it in the small summit pack he borrowed from Deb, he found Deb's space blanket which she had left in the pack. All of a sudden Adrian realized he has gone from no backup to two space blankets and was much happier to face the weather.

Ryan led a descending traverse following some mineral veins across the granite into Polemonium basin below the Polemonium glacier. The face of Sill, with several slippery snow-filled gullies, did not look trivial. We chose the rightmost gully with no snow and headed up. It began to rain and then snow. Clouds touched down on the peaks, and it was cold and damp. Carey pulled out full winter gear with jacket, pants and heavy gloves while Ryan and Adrian watched in envy; they were dressed in their fast and lightweight summer apparel! After Thunderbolt and Starlight, the chute up Sill, although sharply inclined and loose, was comparatively easy going, and we reached the ridge at the same time as the clouds. In a whiteout of clouds and snowflakes, we followed the ridge to the last obstacle, a notch with a couple of Class 5 moves to climb back out of it. We finally reached the summit and the summit box. In the mist, wind, and snow we made a quick summit picture and Adrian signed the register at 1:00 pm, noting that someone had summited the day before. There was no time to search for the earlier entry that Deb and Adrian had made when they summited Sill in 2008 as the second of the 'Climb for a Cure' summits. The clouds began to part, revealing wonderful views of the basin below and the Palisades to the north, piercing through the clouds with their tapered peaks. We descended the way we came and followed Ryan as he made a great climbing traverse to the ridge of Peak 13,900, just 10 feet before the cliffs. We huddled in a sheltered nook under some boulders and enjoyed a lunch of tuna and crackers until we got too cold.

The weather began to improve as we descended to Palisade basin and rounded the corner near Potluck Pass. The rays of light through the clouds playing across the rock and snow was beautiful, and Adrian and Ryan traded leads as they started the long traverse back to Thunderbolt Pass on nasty soft snow and boulder fields, never knowing when to put on or take off crampons. Ryan slowed to a crawl for a while and scared Adrian and Carey who wondered what was wrong with him. He started complaining about his vision, and they wondered if he was being stricken by altitude sickness or was it terminal exhaustion? Nearing Thunderbolt Pass they finally had to stop. Ryan took two Excedrin and laid down under a large boulder. Adrian radioed ahead to Deborah at camp, who also worried. Magically, after a 15 minute rest, Ryan revived. It appeared he had just had a gigantic "bonk"; a little rest and food and suddenly he was ready to move along again. We scrambled tiredly over Thunderbolt Pass and called Deb on the radio to let her know we were approaching camp, but only slowly. After a few minutes Ryan declared he was feeling almost like himself again. Adrian and Carey muttered to themselves about how these young guys recover so fast. However, his recovery may not have been complete as he did concede that maybe Adrian's up-and-down route following the snow from Thunderbolt Pass to camp might have been better than his finely contouring route over boulder field and side slopes of snow. It was our sixth time across this ground and we felt we had earned the right to critique the finest of the route variations. Back in camp, Deborah had hot drinks and food ready, and, although we were relieved that Ryan was totally recovered, we were dismayed that his appetite had returned with a vengeance, as he required Viking-sized portions. Clouds loomed over the horizon, and Deborah announced that another storm was on the way. Ryan declared that it never rains in the Sierras at night, and said not to worry about it. We celebrated a great trip and crawled dog-tired into the tent at 8:30 pm after watching our fill of slanting evening light pour over the Palisade granite walls. That night it rained hard, and although Deborah elbowed Ryan to get up, Adrian was the hardy soul who ran outside to cover all our gear, although he was sure to shake off a few raindrops onto Ryan's head as he lay sleeping. A wet night under nylon had never felt so good.

We awoke at 7:15 am on Sunday, groggy and tired. After a breakfast of all the leftovers we had with the exception of oatmeal, we were able to break camp and leave by 9:40. Ryan was anxious to get back quickly, and offered to pack out all of Deborah's heavier gear with the understanding that she would move along the trail as quickly as possible. The "family points" issue was discussed, and being gone all weekend while your spouse is taking care of all duties with the kids definitely loses family points. Feeling sympathetic that she was losing family points as well, Deborah did her best to sprint across the tundra so that we arrived at Bishop Pass after only an hour of cross country hiking. We were all relieved to be at the point where we would have good trail from there on out. Rapidly descending the switchbacks trail of Bishop Pass we met our first soul in 4 days when we came across a PCT hiker heading in at 11:20 am. We chatted to the trail crew at the base of the pass and were invited to be the first hikers to use their newly constructed trail – quite an honor. We succeeded in a fast hike out in the hot sun to the van, and arrived at 1:10pm. We were grateful that this had been a very successful trip, and our only trip casualty was a pair of rock gloves left behind on Thunderbolt by Deborah.

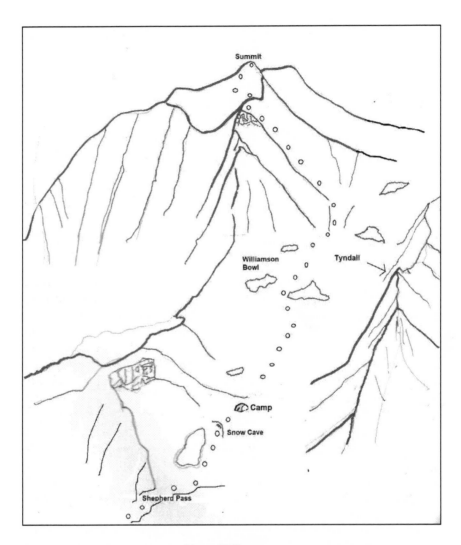

Mount Williamson.

Chapter 10
WILLIAMSON

14,380 feet
May 18th - 21st 2011
Summary: A successful summit during Mother's Day weekend with Spring-like snow conditions.
Our Team: Adrian Crane, Deborah Steinberg, Ray Kablanow, Carey Gregg, Ryan Swehla

On May 20th, 2011, we reached the summit of Williamson at 11:20 in the morning. Strangely, the air was perfectly still and warm on the summit, even though it had been windy and snowing as we climbed the final 1000 feet.

Almost a year ago, we had hiked into Shepherd Pass to climb both Williamson and Tyndall. On that climb, our first Williamson attempt, we were dismayed at the realization that we had climbed up the wrong gully and did not reach the summit. The following day, rather despondent and with "next time bring more 'beta'" ringing in our ears, we set out for Tyndall. Thankfully, we gained the summit of Tyndall ending the dry spell of successful 14er summits. We now returned to Williamson with several sets of trip notes and Ryan, who, having already climbed Williamson, knew the secrets of the correct route (we hoped). We initially also wanted to climb Tyndall again as Ryan still had not visited that summit. Unfortunately, we didn't have the luxury of an extra day for Tyndall so we would have to fit it in as best we could.

We left the van at 9:40 am after getting a good breakfast and picking up permits in Lone Pine. We hiked into the hills along a narrow canyon trail with four stream crossings. The trail turned into a staggeringly long series of zigzags climbing up the sheltered north-facing bowl. At the top of the switchbacks, snow still clung tenaciously to the trail. In the weeks preceding the trip, Deb had been worried about a knee injury, but we were making good progress aided by the fact that the guys were willing to lighten Deborah's load again. Despite the very heavy snowfall in the winter, there seemed to be noticeably less snow than on our first attempt, possibly because we were a week later than last year. We reached the crest of the pass into Williamson Creek at 12:30 and contoured the valley to a nice lunch spot that overlooked the steep and tangled depths of Williamson Creek. We had a simple but satisfying lunch of cheese, crackers and salami. Deborah sacrificed her nice penknife to the mountain gods by accidentally leaving it in the sand at our lunch spot. Ray, the geologist, pointed out interesting rock formations and entertained us with stories of his early days roaming Wyoming with a rock hammer. The trail actually descends 500 feet from our lunch spot as it follows the valley up, altitude that must be regained, and a fact, along with the length and steepness of the route, that contributes to this approach being described as 'dreadful' in *The Climbers Guide to the High Sierra.*

Ryan, Carey, Deborah and Ray on Williamson.

We made better time than last year, possibly because we were not lugging the cumbersome travois with snowshoes as we had previously. We reached Mahogany Flats at 2:45 pm with plenty of daylight and energy left to continue on to Anvil Camp area. Anvil camp is the last nice camping area before Shepherd Pass, but has little in the way of amenities. We stopped at the first water that we found and pitched the tent on snow but next to an area of dry dirt with logs for sitting and cooking. We later found snow-free campsites!

Deborah grumbled to herself that we should have taken the extra time to find a more flat and even-surfaced camping area, but the guys seemed very happy. Every time she fell into a hole or tripped over a rock she worried she would ruin her knees just walking around camp. Fortunately, we were staying there only overnight. Ryan looked through our food supplies and evaluated that we had brought way too much granola and dried fruit for breakfast. Deborah reminded him that everyone grumbled whenever we ate oatmeal. We decided to hang the extra food in a cache to pick up on our descent. In the evening we discussed plans for fitting the Tyndall climb into our schedule. If we got started early and had a good day tomorrow, we might tackle Tyndall in the evening.

We awoke at 5:30 am as the sun rose above the desert mountains to the East, but we enjoyed our morning and lingered, not leaving camp until 7:45. The chance of doing Tyndall was getting smaller. The terrain was covered in snow, so we immediately put on crampons. We made our own way up the valley, occasionally taking cursory glances at the map to see if we could mimic the trail which presumably followed the most sensible line. After a few snowfields, we got into an area of nasty talus. There was a cry just ahead and we all glanced up from our own cautious footsteps to see Ryan face down on a pile of rocks. He had caught his crampon between two rocks and his hiking pole prevented him from putting his hands out, so he landed on his nose and head. Thankfully, he quickly stirred, but when he sat up we saw his face was covered in blood. It looked brutal. After a few minutes of cleaning and bandaging up the wound, Ryan had recovered his breath and we all calmed down. Deborah used a large butterfly bandage to close the gaping wound on Ryan's nose, guaranteeing he would look extra-dorky for a while. Ryan asked if we thought he sounded confused, which would indicate a concussion. "No more than usual," we replied. We were pleased when he responded, "Well if I start making sense you will know that something is wrong!"

We rested for a while, asking him questions about what hurt where, etc., and then discussed the problems of a possible concussion in conjunction with potential altitude sickness. He was unsure whether to continue or go back down, but he had never lost consciousness and was thinking clearly, despite a mild headache. Ryan was concerned about how the altitude would affect his possible head injury, so Ryan went and stood on a high boulder and called his doctor in Modesto! Ryan received a fairly clean bill of health and decided he was OK to continue. It was up to us to make sure he acted no more strange than usual as the day progressed. This was to our advantage because Ryan felt he had to watch his tongue, so he was even nicer than usual. We made our way across car-sized boulders to where we could see the trail peeking through the snow-free side of a large moraine. We followed the trail for a short way before it disappeared again under a snowfield that coated the bottom of a bowl in the moraines. This was the "Pothole." A tent was pitched there, one of the very few signs of people that we saw on the trip. After the four ibuprofen we had given him earlier, Ryan was quickly feeling his old self again, leading strongly up the valley and talking nonsense. Vertical cliffs bounded the north side of the valley and constant rock and ice falls rumbled off the upper slopes and over the cliffs.

Ryan confirms he is OK after a fall on Williamson.

We made good time to the foot of the final steep snow climb to Shepherd Pass, although we were keenly aware that we had lost more time with Ryan's fall, and the chances of a Tyndall attempt had shrunk considerably. We quickly gained the pass and hiked across the wide open plateau to our chosen campsite next to a few boulders with an expansive view to the West. Tyndall towered over us while Williamson stood as a large threatening massif a mile to the south. Deborah declared that with the gorgeous ever-changing view of clouds over Sequoia National Park and the snow cave close by, this was still her favorite campsite and one she had thought of often since last year. It was 12:50 pm, and despite the setbacks, we were in camp well before the 2:00 pm deadline that we had thought was necessary for a Tyndall attempt. Ryan, Ray and Adrian put together the gear they needed for Tyndall, while Deb and Carey got lunch out and started the task of setting up camp while making plans for a hike to the snow cave.

By 1:20 pm, Adrian, Ryan, and Ray were on the way to Tyndall. Deborah called out to be sure to be safe and rope up on the dicey sections. Having climbed Tyndall last year, Adrian wanted to take a different route and headed up the snowfields directly toward a notch about half way along the rocky but level summit ridge of Tyndall. As we climbed, it became apparent that it was quite a steep route and the snow conditions were not ideal. The trickiest was the thin snow cover over steep slabs where crampons skated and ice axes were useless. It was nice to gain the solid rock near the ridge and finally crest the little saddle where we were able to catch our breath. We took in the views on the other side of the ridge and set off along the scramble to the summit. In spite of the predicted low odds of success, it took us just 2 and a half hours to climb Tyndall from camp. When we arrived at the summit block, which overhangs a 1000-foot precipice of the southeast face, Ryan ignored Deborah's admonition to use a rope and leapt onto the block to grasp the very summit. Ray and Adrian took turns doing the same, but using a rope. They radioed down to camp and then took out the summit logs to sign.

On this trip, we brought a long list of friends and family who were cancer survivors or victims, and we added all those names to our entry in the summit log. On the return trip, we didn't fancy the steep ice-and-slabs encounter on our way up, so we continued along the summit ridge and descended on less extreme slopes north of our ascent route. On the last pinnacles of the summit ridge, we encountered some difficult scrambling and were at a loss to figure out how we had avoided it the previous year. Once past the ridge, we descended the bowl to the north for a short distance, cut across the crest in sight of camp, and started the long snowy portion of the descent. Soon, we decided the conditions and slope were good for glissading and slid several hundred feet in the direction of camp. Our return took a mere hour and a half to reach the luxury of a camp, already set up by Deb and Carey with hot water on the boil.

As we prepared dinner, two figures appeared from the direction of Williamson. Adrian, always eager for a little conversation, went to chat with them and find some "beta." They were moving slowly and obviously very tired, and we discovered that these were the two who had camped at the

"Pothole." They had taken the wrong route and were feeling dejected as they struggled back to camp after a long day. They must have done exactly what we did last year and taken the first, not the second, gully that matched the instructions. Later, we joked that they need a sign at the bottom of the gully saying "wrong way to Williamson Summit." Later in the evening, as we continued the usual chore of melting snow for water, we discovered that we had two less cans of fuel than we had intended to pack. Although we reasoned this might necessitate a quick departure after the climb if we ran out of gas, we felt we would be fine for the all-important night before Williamson. Although the weather was clear, it got cold as the wind picked up, so we moved our snow melting operations into the tent. We set ourselves up for an early night and a quick start in the morning for Williamson.

We woke as planned at 4:00 am and started the water heating, anticipating that it always takes us longer than planned to get ready. Nobody wanted to be first out into the cold and snow to stand around and Derek was not with us to set an example. So we all stayed in the tent as we pulled on clothes and found our gear. We ate oatmeal (yes, oatmeal) and a few snack bars and finally coordinated our tumbling exit out of the tent. Ryan did not dare to mention how much he was sick of oatmeal since he had cached most of the granola. Now that we had a reason to get moving, we finished preparations, secured the camp against strong winds, and started across the undulating snow covered terrain toward Williamson by 5:30 am. Very quickly, we were greeted by a beautiful sunrise in the east with pink reflections off Mt. Tyndall to our right. We were all very excited by the lovely full moon looming over Tyndall, and stopped to snap pictures and take videos. Very soon, we reached a high point overlooking the Williamson Bowl and stopped to confirm our route. We descended 400 feet into the basin, crossed an iced-over lake, and wound our way up and down the moraine to the foot of Williamson. Ryan felt confident of the route so we followed him up broken rock. As we passed, we peered scornfully up the misleading gully of the wrong route that had confused our first attempt. After a few hundred feet, the correct gully came into view. We stayed on the rocks as long as possible before putting on crampons and hitting the near-vertical snow slope. While the day had dawned with perfect calm, the weather had worsened during the morning and was now windy and beginning to snow. At the top of the snow and rock chute, we headed for a chimney in the cliffs ahead that Ryan recognized. During the inevitable delay as we roped up and began climbing, we all got cold as the snow and wind intensified. We ended up huddled together on a little ledge beneath a chockstone, all of us complaining about the cold and the chance of being bumped off onto the rocks below. We squeezed under the chockstone, pulled the backpacks up over it, and then completed a short easy pitch to the top of the chimney. We then stepped over the crest onto the wide summit plateau and a whole new view opened up in front of us. We took advantage of a small rock outcrop giving a little shelter from the wind and had a swig of water and a bite to eat before we tackled the final stretch to the top. The last hundred feet were a struggle in the falling snow and icy conditions.

Setting off for Williamson at dawn.

We finally reached the summit at 11:14 am, and found a strange calmness at the top. The wind wasn't blowing and the snow had stopped. Although around us we could see the weather in every direction, we were blessed with placid weather right on the summit, but no visibility to see the views below. We found the summit register, a repurposed ammo box, sitting in the snow. As we had on Tyndall, we copied the list of those for whom we had climbed the mountain and added a few personal comments. After a half hour that passed very quickly, we headed down, retracing our steps across the plateau, and down the chimney under the chockstone. The precipitous snow made for slow going, but soon enough we were below the difficult bits and managed a few short glissades on our way to Williamson bowl. Whether it was the climb of Tyndall the day before or the long day we had already had, we were all tired. Ryan broke away and pushed on toward camp while the remaining four of us gently slogged back in our old tracks. Adrian started thinking about hot tubs, and relayed a story about how one time he and his son Jonathan had a competition over who could run around the hot tub the most times barefoot in the snow after which they would plunge back into the warm water. After a long soak, Johnathan ran around the hot tub 10 times, after which Adrian declared him the winner! Since exhaustion was creeping through our weary bodies, we greatly appreciated the diversion of a story.

When we finally reached camp, we didn't waste much time getting into the tent. We found ourselves dozing off as we cooked and melted snow in the tent. There wasn't much conversation, especially after we passed around a little of Ryan's bourbon. The next morning, we woke early but didn't rush to break camp. Even so, we left camp at 6:50 am, hastened somewhat by a lack of interest in breakfast or water. It did not take long to cross to the head of Shepherd Pass and descend the snow slope to the valley below. We looked forward to our first good water near the 'Pothole' and then stopped again at the Anvil Camp to pick up the enormous bag of granola we had cached there. We left Anvil at 10:45 after a 15 minute halt and reached Mahogany, 1,000 feet lower, in 30 minutes. We didn't even slow down at Mahogany where Ryan took a side trail and had to bushwack back to us when it petered out. Around lunchtime, we looked for our lunch spot, not so much to eat but more so that Deb could look for her knife. Ryan and Adrian passed the time by betting on whether there were two or three saddles on the route. Adrian lost that bet but gained one back when he correctly placed the road to the Bristlecone Pines. We identified the lunch spot, and Ray triumphantly found the knife! We did not hang around and continued, still without lunch. Ryan, Ray and Carey were on a mission, zooming for the trailhead, while Deb and Adrian took it a little more gently, intent on savoring the wilds for a little longer. Everyone made it back to the trailhead by 1:45pm. By the time Deborah and Adrian arrived, Ray had already changed clothes and laid out a tarp for us all to sort our gear.

It was a very excellent adventure, and our twelfth summit for Climb for a Cure. We climbed in honor and memory of many who have suffered with cancer. Deborah climbed in honor of Marie Gallo, as well as her mother Rose Green who, at the time, was still battling the disease. Adrian climbed for his sister Gwen Cottrell, Ray climbed for his friend Judy Brannan, and Ryan climbed for his mother Karen Swehla and mother-in-law Cathie Hoover. At the request of loved ones, we also wrote the names in the summit log of 20 more people who have battled cancer. Despite the difficulty of the climb, it was a good feeling that hopefully our climb may make a difference in the lives of others.

Mount Russell.

Chapter 11
RUSSELL AND SPLIT

14,094 feet (Russell) and 14,065 feet (Split)
August 3rd - 7th, 2011
Also known as "Steep, Stunning, and Spectacular."
Our Team: *Adrian Crane, Deborah Steinberg, Carey Gregg, Ray Kablanow, Christopher Crane, Johnathan Crane, Adrian Bennett, and Josh Boek.*

After many back-and-forth group emails about potential dates and busy schedules, we finally settled on August 3rd through 7th of 2011 to climb Russell and Split. These two mountains are not conveniently located to climb together, but we figured that once we had made the trip over the Sierras we should try to pick up both of the peaks while the going was good. Deborah and Adrian drove across with Ray Kablanow, Carey Gregg, Josh Boek and Adrian Bennett, while Adrian's son Christopher came up from Los Angeles to meet them. Adrian Crane's nephew, Adrian Bennett, lives in Kenya but was in England awaiting the birth of his first child when his mother Barbara encouraged him to come to climb with us, perhaps thinking that once the child was born he might not get many more chances! This trip was especially meaningful to the two Adrians since Barbara was also losing a battle with cancer.

Early in our planning, Deborah had decided to climb in honor of Breast Cancer survivors Jenny Koehler and Loretta Ghaner. With that in mind, she put a call on social media to borrow pink athletic wear suitable for mountaineering, and in came dozens of offers for pink shirts, hats, bandanas, socks, and the like. What she was missing were pink pants. Hmmmm.... pink pants. Where to find pink pants suitable for a mountaineering trip? As it turned out, during a quick trip to Walmart in search of fuel for our stoves, she stumbled upon a pair of pink cropped sweatpants! Oui-laa! Her wardrobe was complete. Now properly suited up in many shades of pink, Deborah was ready to don her backpack and begin slogging uphill. The climb of Russell began at Whitney Portal along the mountaineering route. Having come this way before, we had learned that the best route was to stay right and climb up the North wall by way of ledges. The ledges are rounded and exposed, and they empty out onto a trail a short way from the very beautiful Lower Boy Scout Lake. From there, a talus slope must be climbed, followed by interesting granite slabs up to Upper Boy Scout Lake where we made camp.

Deborah clad in pink as we climb Russell

The weather was beautiful, and as the sun went down it cast pink hues across the cliffs and reflections in the calm waters of the lake. Deborah's pink clothing, in honor of Breast Cancer awareness, cut a dashing figure alongside the sun-tinted cliffs.

Early the next morning, we moved west past the lake following a sketchy path among the talus. In the distance, we could see where the end of the valley ran into the vertical cliffs of Russell. The cliffs were comprised of steep precipices and smooth slabs so we obviously had to cut up to the right to avoid them. Our route to the right was steep and rocky and involved some weaving, traversing and a crawl beneath a huge boulder before arriving about half way up on a rock-strewn bench where the angle of the valley wall became less severe. We turned left again and made a rising traverse towards the cliffs of Russell. Deborah stared anxiously at the smooth vertical cliffs that rose to impossibly sharp knife edge ridges. "Are you sure there is a way up over there?" she shouted. Adrian pulled out a crumpled faded photocopy of a map, lifted his myopic glasses and pulled the page to within 4 inches of his nose. He confidently pointed to where it showed a gully that cut up through the ramparts above, right beside the wall of Russell, and replied "Yes I am sure, we just can't see it yet."

We persevered in our trudge up the rocky slope. In many places, the rocks were small and gravelly, making for slippery tiring progress. Our conversation centered on whether there really could be a gully hidden at the end of the cliffs. Finally we reached the last buttress before the true wall of Russell, and, as we climbed around its lowest cliffs, we could see the fabled gully open up in front of us. "It looks good," yelled back Adrian as he arrived in the gully. The good news was that the gully looked like it would go all the way to the skyline. The bad news was that its sandy and slippery texture required a pace of two steps forward and one step back to move upward.

The gully was bordered by the towering walls of Russell, and led easily, but steeply, to the Russell Carillon saddle. As we crested the top, we came out onto a wide plateau, bright and airy compared to the confines of the gully. We stopped for a rest and let everyone regroup after the physical climb.

A wonderful rock pinnacle graced the ridge, and, since it had a fabulous backdrop of Mt Whitney, we just had to take photos. Adrian Bennet climbed to its tip to provide a splash of color. After the break, we looked at the East Arête leading up to Russell. The East Arête starts off easily enough but soon is whittled down to a sharp granite ridge with impressive drops on both sides. On the left, the sheer cliffs dropped into the valley we just traversed, while, on the right, the curving granite plummeted into the icy and spectacular Tulainyo Lake. At the first sign of difficulties, we roped up into two teams. We traversed west along the knife-like ridge where the route ahead looked always impossibly extreme but at the last minute a way through would emerge. At the head of one particularly steep and loose section, we pulled ourselves over the crest to the east summit, following which, a short traverse brought us to the true western summit. On the way, we glanced down the sheer south side of the ridge which would be our return route. With much excitement and relief, we reached the summit of Russell (#13 for Climb for a Cure). At the very summit, there is a magnificent large cluster of flat rocks that made for the perfect lunch site. With hardly a breath of wind, we lazed in the sun and amused ourselves by looking across at the cluster of ant-like figures on Mt. Whitney summit. We also entertained ourselves by taking turns crawling about the labyrinth of boulders trying to find the items that we accidently dropped between the summit rocks. A carabiner here, a ski pole there. Adrian advised us to never give up hope about finding lost gear as we signed the summit log. Adrian relayed the story about how his son Johnathan once borrowed a rather nice bivy sack for a Boy Scout Snow Camping trip along Highway 108, where he promptly lost it. Adrian and Johnathan returned to the area in summer attempting to find it, but they had no such luck. Meanwhile, five years later, one of Adrian's friends from Kiwanis, Gary Zimmerman, went on a motorcycle trip with friends in that area, where one of the riders found the bivy sack. Knowing that its intended purpose was some sort of camping, but little else, and figuring he had no use for it, he gave it to Gary who was a more outdoorsy kind of guy. Gary held on to it for a few months, and figured he too really had no use for it, but he knew someone who would. At the next Kiwanis meeting, Gary presented the lucky find to Adrian, who exclaimed, "That's my missing bivy sack!"

The summit of Russell was an idyllic spot in these conditions once one forgot about the precipitous drops on every side, but finally we decided it was time to get down. We retraced our steps a few hundred yards to the low point between the two summits. Here, Adrian rigged a single rappel rope and everyone descended 120 feet to the steep talus below. This is actually a class 4 climb but very exposed, so all were happy to rappel. As the last one down, Adrian rearranged the rope as a double rope and set off down knowing the doubled rope would not reach the bottom. Half way down he paused, pulled the rope down and reset it. Once Adrian got down, he unclipped from the rope only to find when he tried to pull the doubled rope down that it was jammed. After a lot of tugging but no success, Adrian left the rope and the group set off down the steep talus heading for the Whitney Russell Pass. The route descends into a bowl on the west side of the Sierra Crest, and then a short climb takes one to the pass to Iceberg Lake. Although it was short, the climb was exhausting as most of us had run out of water and were dehydrated as well as tired. In this bowl, some other climbers, also descending Russell, caught up with us and handed over our neatly coiled rappel rope that they had come across on the way down and retrieved for us. How lucky we were!

Once over the col, we descended snow fields to Iceberg Lake. Here we passed several campsites where Deborah's bright pink outfit was commented upon. While she was very picturesque some of the other climbers probably had trouble taking her seriously, so the rest of our group made efforts to loudly discuss her summit achievements and the fact she was climbing for Breast Cancer research and awareness as we passed their camps. It was late afternoon by now and our group separated as we descended the trail from Iceberg to Upper Boy Scout Lake. It was nearly dark when Deborah and Adrian spied the camp below where somebody was already starting on dinner.

The group on Russell. Ray, Carey, Adrian Bennett, Deborah, Christopher, Josh, Adrian.

The next morning we tried unsuccessfully to get moving early so that we could descend and then drive up to Split Mountain with time to hike in and make a camp ready for a summit the next day. The descent went smoothly as we were beginning to remember the route through the ledges and down the North Fork. We reached the vehicle at Whitney Portal and headed for Split Mountain. But by the time we had had a quick meal, stopped for some supplies and met Johnathan Crane who was joining us on Split, it was getting quite late.

Split Mountain

Adrian's sons, John and Chris, can be characterized as quite adventurous in their own right. Later that year, Chris signed on to row across the Atlantic from the Canary Islands off the coast of Africa to Barbados in the Caribbean as a member of a four-person team. When one rower backed out at the last minute. Christopher, with little effort, was able to convince his brother (who had never before rowed anything other than a canoe) to join him on this adventurous journey of 56 days where their lives revolved around 4 hour shifts; they would row as a pair for 4 hours, then have 4 hours to eat, sleep, and take care of whatever needed fixing on the boat until the next 4-hour rowing shift. They still remain close despite the rigors and confined quarters of that adventure, and it is always enjoyable when one or the other decides to join our team. On Split we were lucky enough to have them both.

Although as the crow flies the Split trailhead appears to be not that far away, it was a time-consuming journey along the numerous miles of rough dirt road to the trailhead and it was 5:00 pm before we reached it. Deborah's demeanor made it clear that we would have to get organized quickly when we hit the trailhead and get hiking before any more time passed.

Despite the late hour, we started out for Split Mountain. We blazed up 4000 vertical feet of elevation toward our base camp at Lower Red Lake, chasing the sun. When darkness arrived, Deborah urged us on, saying we just had to make it to the 10,000 foot level so that we would have a good summit chance the next day. By the light of our headlamps, we navigated the final clusters of willows, never quite sure if we were following streams or trails. When we recognized the lake, we dropped our packs and dispersed in different directions to scout for a good campsite. With each party declaring they had the best place, we finally settled on a location near the lake. Although it was 9:40 pm when we finally arrived at our camp we didn't rush to bed. Everyone was in a good mood and wanted to visit, especially Adrian's sons Johnathan and Christopher and their cousin Adrian Bennett who have climbed together in the past and enjoyed catching up on each other's tales of girlfriends and adventures

When we woke in the morning it was obvious that we had stumbled across the best site in the area even though we couldn't agree on just who had found it. It was a beautiful place in the crisp morning air as we sat on boulders to eat breakfast but soon we were off again. We headed toward the summit of Split Mountain, looking for the most doable route among the snowfields and rock. There were small meadows, a few flowers, and tumbling streams making it a fun and scenic hike. We approached the Sierra Crest which we would cross to get on the west side and climb the north-west slopes to the summit. It swiftly steepened as we approached the crest, and the final 50 feet were a choice of steep snow or rock scrambling. We stayed on the rock and were soon standing in a group on the Sierra Crest with views off to the west as well as the east. The huge expanse of talus leading upward did not look inviting but there was clearly no alternative, so we set off. For a while, we seemed to be making hardly a dent in the ascent of this huge rock field. Then suddenly we looked down, saw our starting point far below, and had the feeling that the rock field was not quite as limitlessly wide as it seemed at the bottom.

Eventually we reached a point where we realized we were "home free," as we could see the rest of our ascent to the summit; only small easy boulders and a little scree. Summit #14 for Climb for a Cure! Just across the namesake horizontal split in the mountain we gazed on surprisingly spectacular pinnacles and cliffs. In the distance to the north and south were trains of mountains. From the summit of Split we could see 12 other fourteeners! We took our time to recount memories of a few of our more challenging climbs, like Starlight, North Pal and Thunderbolt. On the summit were boulders and rocky edges. After a few minutes of catching the view and filling out the summit register, we were all caught in a bout of lethargy.

Deborah was still dressed all in the pink, as she had been the entire trip, and struck a colorful figure on the summit rocks. We wrote the names of several cancer victims in the summit box including Richard Minkkenen who had passed away recently after a battle with cancer. Richard was the brother-in-law of Barbara Miller, a world class runner and dear friend of ours in Modesto, California.

We lounged in clefts in the summit rocks, managing to stay out of the wind and yet in the sun. For Climb for a Cure we had bagged all but one of the fourteener summits. The final peak was to be White Mountain, always listed as the 'easiest' of the California Fourteeners. For Deborah and Adrian, the summit of Split represented something close to the end of the challenge. There was relief, not yet stated aloud, and the first tinges of sadness that it was over. Adrian had already climbed White Mountain, a long, long time ago, so was also able to claim his completion of the California Fourteeners in addition to all the fourteeners in the lower 48 states.

After a long time relaxing and a few naps, we slowly gathered ourselves for the descent. The boulder field which had been such a slog on the ascent, now on the descent allowed us a couple of short glissades on snow patches which was way more entertaining. We all waited on the lip of the Sierra crest for the whole group to arrive and admired the great walls and pinnacles that made up the Sierras in this area. We scrambled down the rock from the Sierra Crest, then descended beside the snow slope. As the steepness relented, each of us jumped on to the snow slope at a place where we were comfortable and slid on down. It was a contented group that wandered into camp that evening where we enjoyed a dinner of anything we could find. Adrian Bennett continued to carve his hiking pole in true Masai warrior fashion.

Deborah and Adrian reminisced again over their many climbs together. On the descent of Mount Shasta Adrian had naively thought we might take a summer to climb these mountains. Deborah had other ideas as to the pace of the project. Eking out weekends from a busy family schedule and enjoying the sights and smelling the flowers as we climbed, we started ticking off the California 14ers. About the only strategic decision we made was that White Mountain, being so easy, should be last so that we could bring a group of friends with us to celebrate our final summit. The California 14ers had indeed turned into a tough and entertaining series of adventures. Winter campsites, technical rock, ice couloirs, long approaches, climbing days that sometimes lasted over 24 hours, deep snow, storms, and defeats made for many memorable peaks. Eventually, after four years, we reached the top of Split

Mountain. All were climbed now except for White. The Palisades with their spectacular and technical peaks had been done. Now we were free to enjoy an easy hike up White Mountain.

The next morning, Christopher hurried out of camp and ran to the trailhead on his way to his next adventure. The rest of us hiked out, engaged in our usual celebratory meal, and returned to Modesto that evening. The whole trip was a fabulous experience, and on the way down Adrian and Deborah reflected on what an amazing journey this has been. We really felt everyone's prayers and encouragement along the way.

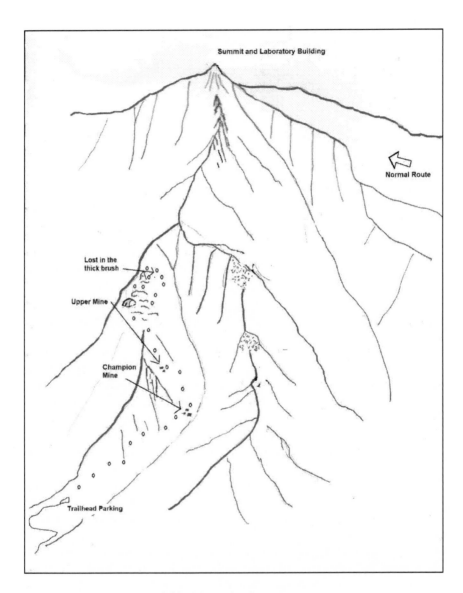

Summit and Laboratory Building

Normal Route

Lost in the thick brush

Upper Mine

Champion Mine

Trailhead Parking

White Mountain winter route.

Chapter 12
WHITE MOUNTAIN IN WINTER

14,252 feet
January 27th-29th, 2012
Also known as "We'll try it in the snow and if it don't go, then we'll try it in the sun....."
Our Team: Adrian Crane, Deborah Steinberg, Carey Gregg, Derek Castle

Among the 15 mountains of over 14,000 feet in California, White Mountain is universally known as the easiest. It is not in the storied and magnificent Sierra Nevada Range; it is in the "White Mountains," a small range to the east of the Sierra Nevada in dry high desert country that consists mostly of rounded high hills. The trailhead is at 11,000 feet unless you care to wait for the right weekend in summer when the gate is opened and you can drive up to 12,000 feet at the Barcroft Station observatory and start your hike from there. Its main claim to fame is not that it hides a hulking central African Gorilla or an abominable snowman, but it merely plays host to a very old tree. The Bristlecone trees on its slopes are admittedly some of the oldest living things on earth which is quite nice, but they only reinforce the sedate reputation of the mountain. After all, what thrill is there in sneaking up on a tree in order to catch a glimpse when it hasn't actually moved in 5000 years!

Nevertheless, it is over 14,000 feet high so it was necessary to visit to complete the California 14er challenge. After 14 summits over four years, we looked back on a tough and entertaining series of adventures, successes, and defeats. All were climbed now except for one. Now we were free to stroll up White Mountain.

It was already late in the year, and we realized that we could not climb White Mountain with our anticipated entourage until the following summer. Deborah suggested that we climb White in winter since it might be a little more of a challenge and having the summit already achieved would take the pressure off when we climbed with the group of friends and family. We needed some winter trips anyway, so we put it on the calendar. We looked up on the internet if there were any trip reports of climbing White Mountain in winter, and amazingly there were none, so this was to be a true adventure!

In January of 2012, we drove across the Sierras on Highway 88 and headed for Bishop, figuring it would make for a faster getaway in the morning and a warmer night if we got a motel room there. We were accompanied by Carey Gregg and Derek Castle, two of our regular partners on outdoor trips. The normal summer route to White Mountain involves driving twenty miles along a dirt road to about 11,000 ft. It is a beautiful road with spectacular views of the Sierras across the Owens Valley, but from late Fall until summer it is closed because of snow. The twenty high-altitude miles are too far to hike reasonably, so we thought the better way in winter would be to tackle one of the little-travelled ridges rising 10,000 feet from the floor of the Owens Valley to White Mountain Summit. As we perused the map that evening we saw that our trailhead, depending on the state of the dirt road and the snow level, would be at about 4,500 ft. That left a lot of vertical to climb. The next morning, we took Highway 6 north out of Bishop. The lone general store supplied us with coffee, and then we took a rough dirt road toward the trail head. We drove as far as we dared on steep rocky roads in Deborah's still-shiny SUV and then set out. We were still a long way below the snow line. Narrow trails across loose steep slopes led us to the lower camp of the old 'Champion Mine' where materials for spark plugs were mined during the world wars. The camp was still in good condition, as volunteers maintain the cabins and make them available to anyone willing to hike the two rugged miles in. One cabin was occupied and the resident insisted on giving us a quick tour of the camp. "I am just staying for a long weekend," he explained. "I and other volunteers come up several times a year. The hike from the trailhead keeps the vandals out so it stays in pretty good condition," he added.

After a quick look at the interesting remains and the slightly renovated cabins, we continued up a poorly maintained, but fun, trail to the upper camp perched in a high side valley. This camp was in much worse shape than the lower camp but was conveniently timed for lunch. We ate inside a cabin, partially sheltered from the keen wind even though the windows were missing and one end hung, half collapsed, over the eroded slopes. We did not put too much confidence in its structural integrity. Opposite was a spectacular cliff honeycombed with mine passages.

After lunch, we climbed upward to a major ridge which we had identified as our best route. We were above the tree line and climbing on an ever fainter trail through brush. This route up the western ridges seemed to be rarely travelled and we had found no trip notes or trail maps. The only existing route led through the abandoned mine, up the gully, until the faint trail evaporated into the dry scrub and snow on the top of the ridge. At least we were on the ridge top though, and we thought surely it must be plain sailing up these ridges as they coalesced and eventually connected with the summit ridge 5000 feet above. We started up the ridge and found that the trees and brush were getting thicker, not thinner, as we climbed.

By late afternoon, we were in six inches of snow, weaving through thick brush and scrambling over occasional rocky outcrops. We halted in a clearing and pitched camp on a perfectly sized snow patch among the willows.

Derek and Carey consider the route on White Mountain.

Once camp was ready and Carey had fired up the stoves, Adrian went scouting. He advanced for a short distance and returned with the report that the brush did not improve and, in fact, became thicker atop more broken rock. On his return to camp, Adrian had had to use the radio to have Derek guide him back as he could see no sign of the tent hidden in the trees. "It is pretty horrible up ahead, but it can't go on like this for long," he said.

As we melted snow for our dinners, we stomped around to keep warm and eyeballed the ridge across the canyon. Although this was a winter trip, we were clearly in a desert, and there had been little snow. We discussed our options. Do you think that looks better over there?" "This ridge seems even rougher up ahead. I hope this brush opens out soon." "Look, we could have taken that line on the other side, and the ridge top over there looks like bare easy hiking," A 50/50 chance of success was agreed on by Derek and Adrian as they lay in the tent that evening.

Part of the 'upper camp' at Champion Mine, White Mountain

The next morning, we set off in the dark at 5:30 am, vowing to spend as long as it would take to make the summit. The only caveat was that Adrian had to catch a plane Sunday evening in San Francisco, so he really did not want to be on the summit at midnight. Immediately, it became a full-contact scramble with large boulders, thin treacherous snow cover, and thick brush. We tried to follow the crest of the ridge and wound through the brush and around rock outcrops in the dark. As dawn turned to daylight, we could see the ridges leading to the summit and eventually even spy the stone building on top. "Boy, that looks a long way away," said Carey. We were moving very slowly. The boulders were spaced widely enough that it was not possible to step from one to the other. The snow cover between hid deep holes and every step was slow and tenuous as we felt for solid ground. When we were not on boulders, we were in thick thorny brush. After two and a half hours we had made a half mile progress. Derek and Ados agreed that the 'summit likelihood meter' was now down to 10%. Our watches never missed a beat; soon it was 10:00 am. We had been traveling for 4 hours and seemed to have made little more progress. With no improvement in the state of the ridge line and only more of the same ahead, our spirits were as low as our "summit likelihood meter." We looked ahead and estimated how many more sections of '4 hours' it would take. "I doubt we will make it by midnight," said Derek. "And then we would still have to get back," Carey added. Deborah egged us on, "Oh, we can make it," Derek and Adrian were not so sure.

The terrain did not let up, and after another hour of struggle we called a halt and discussed our situation. "If we do ever make the summit it will be way late and bitterly cold. I really don't think we can get there from here," Adrian stated. Derek nodded his head either in agreement or acceptance. Carey said "I think we should try the other ridge next time." Deborah added "I think there has to be a better way but I think we should keep going." "So Carey," asked Adrian, "does that mean you are ready to turn around?"

"OK by me," replied Carey.

"Deb, are you OK with that?" asked Adrian, knowing it was 3-to-1 already.

"You know me," said Deborah. "I don't want to go back, but if that is what you all suggest, then it is fine by me. But let's try going back by going lower on the side of the ridge."

We descended a rock rib for a hundred yards and then contoured back along the ridge in brush that was certainly thinner than higher up but involved side hilling on loose rock which more or less evened the score. After a few hours, we approached the level of our camp and headed back up to the ridge crest where our tent would be. Of course, from our new perspective everything was different and it took some time breaking through brush and scrambling up rocks to the ridge crest before we recognized the features that led us back to camp.

We pulled out the stove and stamped our feet to keep them warm as we waited for some water to boil so we could make a hot lunch. While we waited, we discussed where we would go next time.

"I guess we just try the other ridge," said Derek.

"What about the bottom of the canyon?" suggested Carey.

"That looks awfully steep at the end," said Deborah. "I would rather stay to the ridge."

After eating, we hoisted our packs and made our way back through the brush down the ridge descending to the upper mining camp. We took the time to make a quick detour through the shaft that penetrated the mountain and exited in an airy lookout in the middle of a cliff face with a 200 foot drop to the ground. We continued to the lower camp arriving as it started to get dark. Deborah fancied staying the night so we chose our cabins and made dinner on the front stoop. It proved to be a silver lining to the trip to spend a delightful second night on the mountain in the relative comfort of the semi-maintained ghost town cabins.

The next morning was an easy jaunt down to the trailhead. Derek and Deborah followed the canyon down to the lower trailhead while Adrian and Carey followed the trail back to the upper trailhead and drove the Toyota down the steep narrow road to meet the other two. As we slowly drove away, Adrian said "That was a bit harder than I expected. It would be a major epic to get up by that route."

White Mountain, the last 14er for the Climb for a Cure team to summit, proved to be a tough nut in winter. In summer, we knew that it would be an easy walk-up, but in winter it proved to be a fun and physical challenge that got the better of us. We decided to re-group and try it the next winter after the summer event with friends and family.

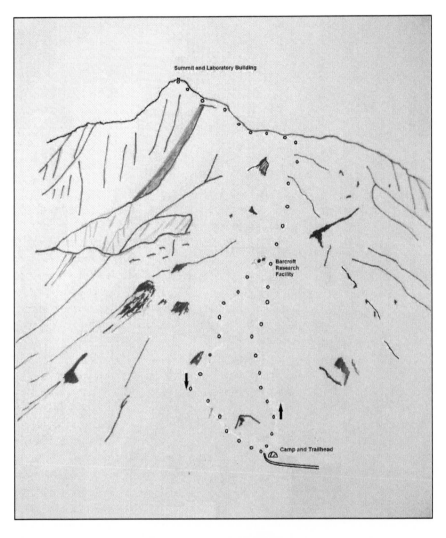

White Mountain normal route.

Chapter 13
WHITE MOUNTAIN IN SUMMER.

September 1st - 2nd, 2012
On our second attempt, we made it up White Mountain and FINISHED THE 14ers!!
Our Team: Adrian Crane, Deborah Steinberg, Carey Gregg, Ross Redding, Karina
Redding, Joanna Warren, Fraser Warren, Sarah Warren, Christopher Crane, Vance
Roget, Brien Crothers, David Spieker, Nancy Barasch. Jenny Koehler and Bruce stayed
at the trailhead.

We always thought that White Mountain would be a meager challenge compared to the rest of the peaks we had already climbed. Our doomed attempt to climb it in winter had started as a way to make White Mountain into more of a challenge. It didn't go too well. Even if we had summited in winter, we planned to climb it again in summer when we could encourage our non-climbing friends to join us. This time, we would go to White Mountain at the right time of year and finish the project. We asked our friends and supporters and rallied a group of fifteen for the trip to climb a 'fourteener' and see the famous Bristlecone Pines.

Those from Southern California and a few who went over early stayed at 4,000 feet in the Bishop area or at 6,000 feet in Bridgeport a little further North. Others coming from Modesto had a Friday night acclimatization camp at 10,000 feet on Sonora Pass. We all then rendezvoused in Bishop at the Danish bakery on Saturday morning. Bishop is the jumping-off point for White Mountain attempts, whether in winter by way of Highway 6 to a trailhead or in summer via Big Pine and the White Mountain Road.

After our fill of fancy coffee and pastries, we drove the 15 miles south to Big Pine, found another few of our group, Chris Crane, Nancy, Bruce and Jenny Koehler, and drove in convoy up the hill out of the Owens Valley and onto White Mountain Road. The road starts off as a twisting asphalt route climbing steadily through the forests. After several miles, just after passing the Schulman Grove of Bristlecone pines, it turns to dirt. We happened to be passing during the ceremonial opening of the Bristlecone Pine Forest Visitor Center so were met with a most unusual traffic jam and parking chaos on this road. Beyond the Schulman Grove, we followed the spectacular ridge at 9,000 and 10,000 feet for 12 miles to the Patriarch Grove which was a bit quieter. Already, Jenny noticed that she was not accustomed to the higher elevation. The route has great views of the Sierra Mountains to the west and the Great Basin and Nevada to the East. We spent a couple of hours visiting the oldest living thing in the world, "The Patriarch," and getting a little active acclimatization by way of a gentle hike around the interpretive trails.

We then continued the 8 miles to the closed gate at the trailhead where we pulled up amongst several other parties who were also planning a climb of White Mountain the next day. It happened that we had arrived on the eve of one of the rare days when the gate will be opened and climbers can drive the two miles to Barcroft Station rather than walk it. "That explains why there are so many people here" said Deborah.

Deborah and Adrian in front of White Mountain.

Adrian's sister Joanna and her children Fraser and Sarah from England were part of the group. Adrian had extolled the beauty and solitude of the California mountains and was now hurriedly explaining why the scene was more reminiscent of a crowded Lakeland car park in northern England than a remote 11,000 foot base camp. "Seriously, on Langley we saw no one for three days," he insisted. Deborah convinced her husband Ross, their older daughter Karina, and her cousin Nancy to join on this trek up the mountain. Also special about this trip was that six people who were on our original winter climb of Mt. Shasta, which sparked our quest to climb the rest of the 14ers, were with us today.

We pitched several tents for camp and arranged cooking on vehicle tailgates. We discussed whether we should take advantage of the gate being opened in the morning and almost all decided we should hike the whole way. It soon got cold and a breeze sprang up, reminding us that we were at a great altitude. The grand and leisurely evening meal that we planned was eaten hurriedly and everyone went to bed. A huge moon rose over our camp.

Adrian was determined to be a good host and the next morning, after he awakened at 4am, he lay nervously eyeing his watch until 5:15 when he got up and started heating water for our large group. Around dawn, the gate on Barcroft Road was opened, and a small convoy of cars set off. It is a truism of large groups that everything takes a long time, but the morning chill discouraged any dawdling and we were soon ready. After the rigors of their night at high altitude, Jenny and Bruce confirmed that they could not make the hike and decided to stay close to trailhead and cars.

Carey led the rest of us from camp, following a faint trail along the old road. Adrian's sister Joanna started slowly, giving herself time to warm up. Before long, the group was spread out, hiking at their own pace. The route was obvious and everyone regrouped after two miles when we rejoined the dirt road at the Barcroft Research Station. Ross and Nancy joined us there having driven up. We climbed the rough trail behind the cluster of buildings and equipment that make up the Barcroft Station and crested a ridge, greeted by views of the summit slopes across a wide plateau. The slopes were a striking yellow shade compared to the grey of the surrounding rocks. Nearby was the old observatory building, a small round structure with a domed roof. We hiked across the plateau and Joanna felt her condition worsen. The group encouraged her on, but eventually she was ready to stop. Christopher, her nephew, generously agreed to stay back with her. Vance rooted in his small pack and pulled out some caffeine pills and other horse medicines that he urged her to try. We started on the climb up the final slopes, and after a few hundred feet looked back to see Joanna and Chris heading our way and gaining! After a long slog up the slopes, the whole group made it to the summit, arriving in dribs and drabs.

The weather on the peak was sunny but windy, and the first arrivals took shelter behind the building until all were present. Our final summit saw an extended celebration and a lot of picture taking. A bottle of bubbly appeared. Adrian opened it and lightly sprayed the group before taking a small swig. Deborah threw back a big taste and then doubled up in laughter as it came out of her nose. High altitude and sparkling wines make for a fun celebration.

Writing in the summit book was both a happy occasion, yet very solemn.

Deborah was reminded of her friend Kristen Machado who was near the end of her losing battle with cancer, and was the first person for which she had climbed. Deborah and her family also remembered her mother, Rose Green, who, in the middle of the Climb for a Cure Project, had acquired Merkel Cell Carcinoma and passed away in 2011. Deborah's cousin Nancy wrote in the summit book about her late husband Richard, and Adrian wrote about his siblings who had passed. After writing in the summit book, we all set off down the mountain with many memories of our loved ones who battled cancer still fresh in our minds. Some rushed ahead to try and get back home the same evening while others moved more gently, planning on camping again near the trailhead and preferring to savor the moment.

Some of our large group on White Mountain.
Back row: Adrian, Brien, Deborah, Ross, Karina, Fraser, Sarah, David.
Front row: Vance, Carey, Nancy, Christopher, Joanna

Thirteen of us summited White Mountain on Sunday September the 3rd, 2012 to complete our quest of climbing all of the California 14ers for Climb for a Cure supporting STOP CANCER and funding for Cancer research. For Deborah and Adrian, this was their 15th 14,000-foot summit in California, and the completion of their mission!

We took a moment to recognize the six members of the climbing party who were on the original winter climbing trip of Mt. Shasta that launched Climb for a Cure: Carey Gregg, Chris Crane, Brien Crothers, Vance Roget, Adrian, and Deborah.

We had expected White Mountain to be an easy stroll, but it proved to be a not-so-easy 14-mile round-trip. Because of the altitude we moved slowly but all thirteen of us reached the hot and dry summit, although it took five hours. White Mountain proved to be a satisfying final mountain.

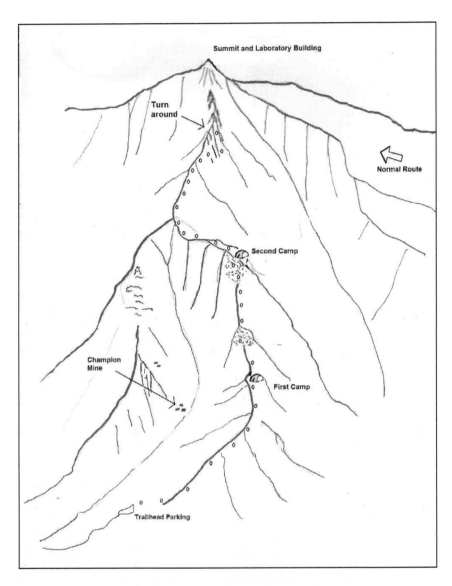

White Mountain winter route (again).

The Truth Zone

Chapter 14
POSTSCRIPT.

White Mountain just cannot get any respect.

Neither Deborah nor Adrian thought of this 14ers project as a one-time foray into the outdoors. Both had been active in the outdoors, and while they hoped the project would lead them to new places and maybe occasionally push the limit neither had thought of it as the capstone or end of their outdoor careers. The four years of the project had proved to be an intense time with so many hard trips, new places, and great friends. But after the final ascent of White Mountain, there was still one piece of business undone. We had not succeeded on a winter attempt of White Mountain. Perhaps we hadn't pushed hard enough, perhaps had used the excuse of running out of time. Perhaps we were just unlucky with our route choice. That would have to be corrected, how hard could it be?

White Mountain just cannot get any respect. Even after our aborted winter attempt and what turned into a long day even in summer, we were not ready to concede that it was a tough peak. In whispered conversations we planned a winter re-match.

Six months later in January of 2013, we found ourselves back in a motel in Bishop with 8 friends. The group drove up to the 4,500 foot trailhead and started out once again for White Mountain. This time we followed the valley floor for a short way and then turned to climb to the south wall of the canyon. It was a difficult struggle up the steep loose slopes. Eventually, they leveled off and we found ourselves in a forest of low trees. A gentle rain began. We meandered through the trees and by late afternoon found ourselves at a flat area at the foot of a steep rocky ascent. After a discussion, we voted to make camp rather than start up the ascent that we could see rising above us in the mist. The fog cleared and that night we had beautiful views as we sat around a campfire.

We woke to mist and enveloping clouds. Ahead of us we saw just the first 100 yards of the steep rocky climb. We started up, each taking whatever route seemed to be easiest. At one wondrous point we sensed brightness. We stopped and turned to see the misty forms of our climbing partners just below while just above them we looked over the clouds to see the peaks of the Sierra Nevada 50 miles away across a cloud-filled Owens Valley. As each climber emerged from the mist they were highlighted in the bright sunlight with a backdrop of mountains above a sea of cloud. We paused for endless photos. Soon we reached the top of the steep rocky slope and found a low angled ridge. The rocky crest of the ridge and the brush encroaching from each side made for an entertaining hike.

Heading up White Mountain with cloud across the Owens Valley and the Sierra Crest in the distance.

We stopped for lunch on one rocky promontory, admiring the views of the mountain side above the cloud. The snow was now thicker, and in the afternoon warmth of the sun the snow had softened, necessitating the use of snowshoes. Our route generally followed the ridge but its crest was often a fin of rock and we swerved from side to side as we climbed. At last, we gazed along a level stretch of easy ridge. It was late afternoon and we stood in the last group of trees. Beyond was only bare snow and rock open to wind and weather. We decided to make camp in the lee of the scattered trees in this last grove. While a cold wind blew we gathered by a small fire and enjoyed our stunning camp perched on the ridge. In the starlight we could see or sense the ridges leading up to White Mountain summit. "We can see almost all the way. Tomorrow's going to be a good day," said Adrian.

We set out just before dawn the next morning. The snowy ridge resolved into detail as the sun came up, and we followed it to the bottom of a sharp lengthy ascent. At the top, the ridge leveled out a little but became rockier. We contoured around a pinnacle to turn onto the west side. The ridge above us narrowed into a rocky spine. Our contouring route crossed a few ribs and increased in slope. We crossed a couple of snow gullies and reached a steep rocky arête that we did not fancy crossing. We halted in a steep gully of loose rock. It was very uncomfortable, airy and loose. Chris Crane climbed to the ridge top but returned with the news that the ridge looked pretty tough. Jack Styer had stayed on the ridge crest and we were not sure where he was. In light of Chris Crane's news and our already precarious situation we chose to retreat. We retraced our route over steep gullies and icy snow slopes. Over our shoulders we could see the summit of White Mountain but in the thousand vertical feet between us were a narrow ridge and steep rock faces. "Wow, this is quite a problem," said Ray Kablanow. "It seems like such an easy mountain; there must be a way to climb it in winter," replied Deborah. "Well, we have plenty of time to try again," laughed Adrian.

We reluctantly turned around and retraced several tricky rope lengths to easy ground. We reached camp just before dark and started the stoves for the evening meal. As dusk fell we watched the stars come into view over the high ridges and wondered where Jack Styer was. Eventually someone pointed out a dim headlight on the far ridge. As it approached it became brighter and while we knew Jack was probably having a miserably cold trip back to camp at least we knew he was safe, although he looked terribly dejected as he too did not reach the summit, but not for lack of trying.

As we descended the mountain the next day we debated why it was so tricky. Looking around from high on our ridge we viewed the other possible routes. "Now I understand why there are no trip reports for White Mountain from the west – no one does it!" said Deborah.

Finally, White Mountain, as if it cared, had our respect.

EDITOR'S NOTE: Citing "unfinished business" Adrian and Deborah did finally make it to the summit of White Mountain, in winter from the west side, using a slightly more southerly ridge on December 6, 2020.

ACKNOWLEDGMENTS

The pursuit of the California 14ers has been a wonderful enterprise. We found that we managed to achieve a goal largely because of the motivation by and help of others. There were many that encouraged and supported our efforts, but as a tiny team on a mountain, our friendship and companionship were crucial to our successes and made the journey so much more worth the suffer-score. There were many moments when the lives of our friends were dependent on our own actions and we took that job seriously. However the emotional support we gave each other was equally as important. They say that "What doesn't kill you makes you stronger," and we have all grown from this quest. It has been an honor to climb in memory of victims of cancer whose struggle is so much harder than any of our efforts in the mountains. It has been humbling to realize how many are personally stricken and to realize that every single one of us is affected by having friends and family members suffer. During this quest, both Deborah and Adrian lost close family members to cancer. We have felt guilty that we have been able to enjoy the mountains and great friendships through the 14ers project. We hope that we have raised some awareness and funds toward cancer research.

Thank you to everyone for their support and interest in our project and in Climb for a Cure (www.climb14ers.org). We have all been touched by this terrible disease and witnessed the suffering of relatives and loved ones. Deborah and Adrian believe that basic research will help find cures for cancer, and that is why we had chosen to support STOP CANCER. Recently STOP CANCER closed its doors after 30 years of funding Cancer Research. We urge our readers to support City of Hope whose Cancer Centers also support groundbreaking Cancer Research https://www.cityofhope.org/. We truly hope that in our lifetime a cure for cancer is found.

Deborah and Adrian would like to acknowledge the many people who supported our quest to climb the California 14ers and prayed for our safety during each climb.

Deborah would like to acknowledge her husband Ross, who patiently stayed home taking care of school and household duties while his wife was off climbing mountains. She sees the bravery and independence of her daughters Karina and Erin, and wonders how much is due to the fact they watched their mother head off into wild and challenging territory, and is grateful that they also both love the outdoors. She is grateful for the angels on her shoulder, the many people who have battled cancer watching over her in the many scary and airy moments on the climbs. She is grateful for her friendship with Adrian and the many others who joined, who believed she could do it, even when she did not believe in herself.

Adrian would like to acknowledge his Uncle Hol and father Charles who introduced him to the mountains a long time ago and taught him the skills to survive in them. Also, given that the great adventures of climbing and authorship both require dedicated and selfless support, he deeply thanks his wife Karen who never resisted his leaving and always welcomed him home. He also thanks his boys Johnathan and Christopher who showed by their interest and participation that they supported his efforts. He is grateful for the rotating group of friends who never let them feel they were alone on their trips. He thanks his friend Deborah who never let failure be an option. He thanks every one of them.

TIMELINE.

Peak	Date	Note	Climbers
Mt Shasta	February 15th -18th 2008	Success on Mt. Shasta in winter but great weather.	Adrian Crane, Deborah Steinberg Derek Castle, Carey Gregg, Brien Crothers, Ray Kablanow, Vance Roget, and Mark Richardson, Christopher Crane, Johnathan Crane, Melissa Griffith, Griff Griffith, Brian B.
Mt Sill	July 30th August 3rd 2008	Success on Mt. Sill and attempt on Polemonium Peak	Adrian Crane, Ray Kablanow, Mark Richardson, and Deborah Steinberg. We were joined for part of the way by Lewis Ase and his girlfriend Carey Pivcevich and their dog Bruno.
Middle Palisade	Sept 10th – 14th 2008	Success on Middle Palisade but never got near Split!	Deborah Steinberg, Adrian Crane, Ray Kablanow, Christopher Crane and, as camera guy, Rick Baraff.
Mt Whitney and Mt Muir	November 20th - 23rd 2008	Cold weather success on Whitney and Muir.	Adrian Crane, Deborah Steinberg, Ray Kablanow, Derek Castle, Carey Gregg and Rudolphe Jourdaine.
Mt Langley	March 13th - 15th 2009	Victory snatched from the Jaws of Defeat on Langley. Our only trip where we used bicycles.	Adrian Crane, Deborah Steinberg, Ray Kablanow and Carey Gregg.
North Palisade and Polemonium Peak	July 29th August 2nd 2009	Success in the Palisades: North Palisade and Polemonium but alas Starlight was not in the cards this trip.	Adrian Crane, Deborah Steinberg, Ray Kablanow, Ryan Swehla with assistance from Jack & John Styer on July 29.
Split	January 14th -17th 2010	Failed winter attempt of Split Mountain - Tough, tough and tougher...	Adrian Crane, Deborah Steinberg, Carey Gregg, Derek Castle and Ryan Swehla.
Williamson and Tyndall	May 12th – 16th 2010	Oh so close on Williamson but we did make Tyndall.	Adrian Crane, Deborah Steinberg, Ray Kablanow and Carey Gregg.
Thunderbolt and Starlight	July 7th - 11th 2010	Success! Also known as "I can't believe we did that...."	Adrian Crane, Deborah Steinberg, Ryan Swehla and Carey Gregg.
Williamson	May 18-21st 2011	Did you bring the trip notes? Yes! We made it!	Adrian Crane, Deborah Steinberg, Carey Gregg, Ray Kablanow and Ryan Swehla.

Russell and Split	August 3rd - 7th 2011	Steep, stunning and spectacular success on Russell. Then on to the summit of Split	Adrian Crane, Deborah Steinberg, Carey Gregg, Ray Kablanow, Christopher Crane, Jonathan Crane, Adrian Bennett, and Josh Boek.
White Mountain in Winter	January 27th-29th 2012	Also known as "We'll try it in the snow and if it don't go, then we'll try it in the sun....."	Adrian Crane, Deborah Steinberg, Carey Gregg, Derek Castle
White Mountain	September 1st- 2nd 2012	Summer group summit of White Mountain and we FINISHED THE 14ers!	Adrian Crane, Deborah Steinberg, Carey Gregg, Ross Redding, Karina Redding, Joanna Warren, Fraser Warren, Sarah Warren, Christopher Crane, Vance Roget, Brien Crothers, David Spieker, Nancy Steinberg-Barasch, Jenny Koehler and Bruce.

PEAKS RANKED BY DIFFICULTY.

Our subjective ranking by difficulty.

Peak	Altitude (ft)	Notes
Starlight	14,220	Long and technical with a tricky summit
North Palisade	14,242	Long and technical
Thunderbolt	14.003	Technical with a tricky summit.
Polemonium	14,100	Technical
Middle Palisade	14,012	Long and scrambling, some tricky sections
Russell	14,088	Long and scrambling, airy knife ridge
Williamson	14,375	Long and scrambling
Tyndall	14.018	Long and scrambling
Mt Sill	14,153	Long and scrambling
Mt Muir	14,012	Scramble
Mt Shasta	14,162	Long and snowy
Split	14,058	Poor trail
Mt Langley	14,026	Poor trail
Mt Whitney	14.495ft	Good trail
White Mountain	14,246	Good trail (the easy way)

PEAKS RANKED BY HEIGHT.

Peak	Altitude in feet	Altitude in meters
Mt Whitney	14.495 *	4418
Williamson	14,375	4381.5
White Mountain	14,246	4342
North Palisade	14,242	4341
Starlight	14,220	4334
Mt Shasta	14,162	4316.5
Mt Sill	14,153	4314
Polemonium	14,100	4297.5
Russell	14,088	4294
Split	14,058	4285
Mt Langley	14,026	4275
Tyndall	14.018	4272.5
Middle Palisade	14,012	4271
Mt Muir	14,012	4271
Thunderbolt	14.003	4268

* Being reconsidered as 14505ft high.

BLISTER PREVENTION.

Blister Prevention (Deborah's method).

As mentioned in chapters of this book several times, my skin is terribly susceptible to blisters, especially when I am carrying a heavy backpack. Although we took a picture of my heels when we returned from Mt. Sill, I have decided not to share it, because it could cause a trigger reaction in some individuals, so let us all just agree, it was not pleasant. I had brought the usual moleskin, etc., but for me it was not helpful. On that trip Mark Richardson, a seasoned adventure racer, suggested John Vonhof's book *Fixing Your Feet* which I read from cover to cover when I returned. His book includes a lot of good information for athletes who can be brutal on their feet during endurance events. John emphasizes pre-taping your feet and trial and error, but I would like to share with you my particular method that really helped me, as it may help others in my situation.

So for me, if I am not prophylactic, I am in trouble. It is super important for me to have my feet taped and lubed BEFORE we hit the trail. From experience I have found that I can prep the night before, as the taping takes time, but I need to leave my liner socks on. My experience is once you remove the liner sock the pads and tape release with it, and you need to re-tape. If you can handle not removing your liner socks for a few days, I have found the taping will last about 3 days in a pinch. The other thing that is important is pre-testing your sock combination with your boots or shoes that you will wear before your big trip. In my situation, my feet will swell a bit once I am at altitude, so I have to adjust my calculations while testing out socks to allow a little room for that.

What ended up working best for me in almost all of my boots was a very thin polyester liner sock covered by a thin synthetic non-binding hiking sock. The brand of hiking sock I currently wear is Wigwam, but I have worn other hiking socks on the thinner side that are non-binding. Ironically, for long-distance running I have not had as much issue with blisters, and have found I don't always need the full method below which has been the most helpful for backpacking and mountaineering trips.

Okay, what follows is my exact method, and my hope is to banish the misery of blisters on your next outing!

You will need in your kit:
- Very sharp scissors (mine are foldable)
- Alcohol Prep Wipes
- Tincture of Benzoin (see notes)
- Cotton Swabs
- Hydrocolloid Bandages (I use CVS Advanced Healing)
- 2 –inch wide tape (see notes)
- Lubrication (see notes)
- Zip bags

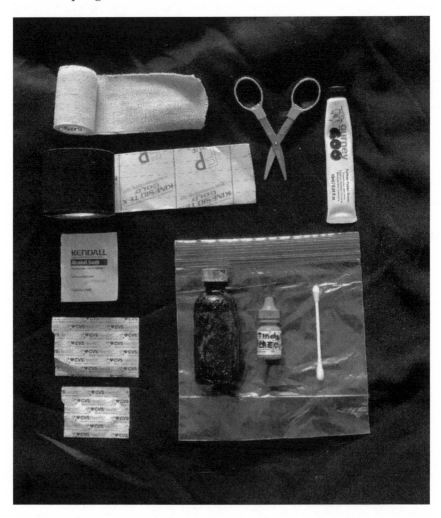

Deborah's Blister kit

Tip: If applying this process to the back of the heel, be sure to flex your foot during the entire application process. The first thing I do is clean my foot with alcohol wipes wherever I am to apply bandages or tapes, which removes skin oils which reduce adhesiveness. This photo comes from my own cupboard, and I included my bottle of Tincture of Benzoin instead of a shiny new bottle to relay a point: it is messy! It is also hard to find, and I had to special order mine, but it can be purchased through REI or Adventure Medical Kits in smaller quantities. I purchased a large bottle, but before long trips I fill a small container to bring. It has a tendency to leak out of whatever container I use and is sticky. Therefore I recommend carrying it in its own plastic bag with cotton swabs. Although originally developed to treat canker sores and skin fissures, it is mostly used these days by athletes as a pre-adhesive, and allows bandages to stick much better. After the alcohol has dried on my feet I apply a layer of Tincture of Benzoin with a cotton swab to an area no larger than where my tapes will be applied. For the back of my heels that means applying a layer 2 inches wide and 3 inches long, while keeping the foot flexed. After the tincture of benzoin has dried somewhat and is tacky to touch I apply a hydrocolloid bandage. For the heel, there are several ways to apply depending on your problem area. From experience I have found that one large bandage applied vertically on the heel to be sufficient, but I have also used two large bandages stacked horizontally. I also use the smaller bandages for other problem areas like the "bunion area" at the big toe joint. Always have on hand extra supplies for an endurance event in case of problems. After applying the bandages I find it most helpful to apply tape over the top of it. This helps prevent the bandage from coming off for the long haul. My favorite is Elastikon tape, but I have found Kinesio Tex Gold to work well also, and is easier to find. Tip: Always round the corners of your tape before applying. I usually cut a 3 inch long piece of 2 inch wide tape for my heels, round the corners, and then apply to my still flexed heel. Be sure to press firmly along the edges to help seal the tape on your foot. After all this I apply a thin layer of lubrication over the bandages. In a pinch you can use petroleum jelly, but there are many anti-chafing commercial products available. I like Gurney Goo, which I also apply between my toes. Another area to which I will apply this method is to the ball of my foot which often will blister on long downhills.

Now to apply your socks: Apply them VERY CAREFULLY, to avoid pulling on the bandages. As mentioned previously, I always apply a thin liner sock first, and wear a thicker hiker sock over that.

Of course there will be trial and error for what works best for you, but my goal is to shorten the learning curve!

Blister Prevention (Adrian's method).

• Apply socks, matching preferred but unnecessary.
• Apply boots/shoes. Lace tying preferred but again not necessary.
• Hike.

FOOD PLANNING FOR MOUNTAINEERING.

Although many seasoned adventurers would be tempted to skip this addendum, it may provide useful experience for those who plan outdoor trips with more than a couple of people. For our trips, Deborah was usually the one relegated to plan, purchase, and organize the food that we would carry for the entire trip and this is her advice.

Amongst our regular participants no one has any specific dietary restrictions which simplifies things. Once in a while we would have along a vegetarian, someone with a specific dietary issue, or a picky eater, and they would tell us ahead of time that they would do their own food. I tried to make as few trips as possible to procure our food and I almost always went to the bulk food section of our local grocery store, Winco, and to Trader Joes. Along with our food I usually bought a supply of zip bags to re-package our food. Once home I set about removing cardboard boxes and unnecessary packaging, and sorting the food into piles of appropriate portions of Breakfast, Lunch, Dinner, and Snacks.

Our group is very weight-conscious, meaning the food itself cannot be heavy or else it would get left behind in the truck! We are usually carrying several days' worth of hiking and climbing gear and although that big bag of tangerines looks appealing, it is not practical. Where we made somewhat of an exception was for the first day's lunch. Typically for the first day you have a heavy load and it is a bit of a treat to start out with good food. Plus you don't have to carry it too far. Our typical first meal is on the trail after hiking about 4 hours when everyone is pretty much ready for a Lunch break. For this we do usually break out a fresh avocado, brie cheese, a tomato, and crackers. Other good lightweight choices for lunch are individual packets of peanut butter shared among all (usually Jif), dry salami, and dehydrated fruit. Freeze dried fruit (as opposed to traditionally dried fruit) is the most lightweight, deliciously crunchy, and available at Karen's Naturals or Trader Joes. The easiest to find are apples, bananas, strawberries and mango. We always brought bananas, because the potassium helps prevent muscle cramps at night from electrolyte loss. The weight savings of freeze dried fruit and vegetables is well worth the extra cost. If it is a winter trip and we do not have to worry about spoiling food, we also bring Canadian bacon.

For dinner rarely did we cook in a pot, because we were usually too tired to either cook or do the dishes! We almost always had traditional Add-Hot-Water Backpacker's meals available at REI, Dick's, and other sporting goods establishments. The two most common brands are Mountain House and Backpacker's Pantry, and we would typically order a season's worth of the 4-person meals whenever available. Unless we had someone with a big appetite with us (ours was Ryan), we allocated 1 regular serving per person, however we supplemented dinner with a few add-ons: We almost always brought one or two packets of different flavors of Idahoan brand mashed potatoes per dinner, and found that we could pour it into our empty Mountain House dinner bag, add boiling water, stir, and eat almost instantly. We also usually had a ramen cup of soup or at least chicken bouillon available that we would supplement with dehydrated vegetable flakes and dehydrated chives. We often started dinner with instant hummus (available in the bulk section of Winco) and crackers for which we had to bring a small container of olive oil and lemon juice. Another instant dinner dish is couscous. You add boiling water and just let it sit until it is ready. Couscous is another dish where you could add extras like dehydrated chives and vegetables and bouillon to make it very tasty. To top off dinner, when we remembered, we often brought a small container of alcohol of some sort, usually enough for a taste per person for a night or two.

Before we broke out the alcohol, we tried to prep for the next day. We have very lightweight nylon string bags of different colors that we found most convenient for keeping, hanging (when necessary), and finding our food. We would sort out what we wanted to take for lunch and snacks for the next day, and separate it in a bag, so it was ready to go or distribute for the next day. All our breakfast stuff was in the "Blue for Breakfast bag", so it was ready to go for the morning. We typically brought Starbucks instant 'Via' coffee, instant creamer, tea, hot cocoa packets, freeze dried fruit and oatmeal and/or granola and freeze-dried milk. In the granola I usually added chopped almonds and dried cherries or cranberries.

I also had a bag of snack bars, a bag of almonds, raisins, and dried fruit, and an individual bag of cookies (which always included Oreos) for each person.

Following is our mountaineering food planning list which is by no means infallible but is a good starting point.

Item	Our Allocation per average person	Notes
Breakfast:		
Starbuck's Vias	1 per drinker per day	+ a few extra. "Cowboy Coffee" works too, but takes more room.
Instant Creamer	2 tsp per user per day	
Tea	1 teabag per drinker per day.	Shared around
Hot Cocoa	1 – 2 per person per day	We tried not to run out!
Instant Oatmeal	2 packets per person per day	We got sick of Oatmeal daily
AND /OR Granola + milk	½ cup per person per day	The Granola option is much heavier, but a lot tastier. I always added chopped almonds and dried fruit.
Instant Dry Milk	1 1/3 cups dried milk per 4 cups water makes about a quart.	
Freeze Dried Fruit	½ cup per person per day more or less	Available at Trader Joes or Karen's Naturals.
Lunch:		
Crackers	Approximately ¾ cup of crackers per person per day.	Usually for a group of 4, 1 package per day.
Cheese	2 - 3 oz per person per day	1 oz is about the size of your thumb for reference. We usually brought something fancy for the first day, like Brie
Peanut Butter	1 individual Jif Packet per day for our group	
Canadian Bacon (Winter trips) or Dry Salami	2 slices per person per day on average	Usually 8 oz of this stuff goes a long way, and it is heavy.
Avocado		Usually 1 avocado for the beginning of the trip to share

Tomato		Usually 1 for the beginning of the trip to share.
Freeze Dried Fruit	½ cup per person per day more or less	Available at Trader Joes or Karen's Naturals

Snacks:

Almond Raisin Dried Fruit Snack Mix or GORP	½ cup per person per day is usually sufficient	
Snack Bars	2 per person per day	
Cookies and Oreos	I usually allocate 1 baggie full per person, which is about 6 cookies, per trip	I honestly don't know why I do it this way, but everyone gets their own baggie to hoard or share!

Dinner:

Mountain House or Backpacker's Pantry Freeze-Dried Meals	1 serving per person per day	4 Person meals are most efficient use of space.
Package of Idahoan Mashed Potatoes	1 package per night per trip	Pour into empty Mountain House container, add 2 cups boiling water, stir, ready in one minute.
Cup of Noodles or Bouillon	1 – 2 per person per night	Add dehydrated vegetables and chives to Bouillon, add hot water, dissolve and stir.
Instant Couscous	If bringing, plan on ½ to ¾ cup per person cooked couscous	1 cup dry couscous makes 2 – 2 ½ cups cooked couscous
Instant Hummus	I typically bring 1/2 cup to 1 cup dry per trip if we are not tight on weight.	If bringing you must bring olive oil and lemon juice in a small waterproof container to mix with it.

GEAR CHECKLIST.

(W) = for Winter trips only, (S) = for Summer trips only

Essentials:
Tent
Sleeping Bag
Air Mattresses
Backpack
Head lamps
Compass/Map
Phone
Phone charging device
Hiking boots
Pocket Knife
Matches
Gaiters
Extra batteries
Water filter
Walkie Talkies/Radios
Fanny Pack
Water Bottles
Hydration Pack (not ideal on winter trips)
Bug Repellent
Camera
Whistle necklaces
Walking sticks
Trash Bag/Pack Cover
Sudoku crossword and/or Book

Personal Items:
Sunscreen
Toothpaste
Deodorant
Camp Soap
Toilet Paper/Wipes
Hand shovel
Hand Sanitizer
Chapstick
Brush/Comb
Blister stuff
Medicines/Vitamins
Sharp scissors
Neosporin
Hydrocortisone
Band Aids
Sunglasses
Contact lenses/solutions

Clothing:
Pants
Shorts
Bandanas/buff/barkie
Warm Shirts
Cool Shirts
Sun Hat
Underwear
Socks
Flip Flops (S) or Down Booties (W)
Down jacket
Rain Poncho/Windbreaker
Warm hat
Long Underwear

Cooking/Eating:
Stove/Jet Boil
Pots & Pans (dependent on stove)
Fuel. (If using butane/isopropane bring 1 450ml can per 5 person days if running water available or 1 can per 2 person days if melting snow for water.)
Plates, Cups, Utensils
Ziplock Bags
Bear canister
Food: See Separate Food Planning Section

Climbing: (for all Technical Trips)
Crampons
Ice axe
Harness/ Carabineers /ATC
Rope
Daypack/Summit Pack
Map/Guide
Helmet
Rock gloves
Pro-gear and Slings
Supergaiters (for Deep Snow and winter only)(W)
Snow Shoes (W)

ABOUT THE AUTHORS

Adrian "Ados" Crane set the speed record for climbing all of the 14ers in Colorado in 1993, well before beginning this lofty adventure of climbing all of the 14,000 foot peaks in California. However he has climbed, run, hiked, and adventure raced in many of the most glorious places in the world, and competed in every Eco-Challenge Race including Eco Fiji 'The Worlds Toughest Race' and four Raid Gauloises: Argentina 1995, South Africa 1997, Tibet 2000, and Vietnam 2002. In 1999 Adrian founded Gold Rush Adventure Racing, where he remains Race Director. During his races and travels he has found  people everywhere to be unfailingly kind and positive, whether it is someone from a small village in Tibet, or a large city in Kenya. Adrian is a computer programmer by trade and is married with two adventurous sons who have climbed Denali and Rowed the Atlantic. Adrian lives in Modesto, California with his wife and her many cats. Climb for a Cure has great meaning to Adrian, who lost a brother and sister to cancer. Adrian's other book: is 'Running the Himalayas' (Richard & Adrian Crane, 1984)

Deborah Steinberg is an Optometrist in Modesto, California who enjoys just about any outdoor activity that puts her in a natural setting. She is not afraid to latch onto others' well-made plans, which has allowed her to participate in some incredible adventures, including climbing all 15 of the mountains in California over 14,000 feet. She is married to a very loving and tolerant husband who knows it is futile to stop his wife when she has a goal. Her two daughters enjoy the outdoors as well, which their mom insists has made them  strong and independent young women. At the beginning of this quest to climb the California 14ers in 2008, Deborah had no family history of cancer, however since that time she lost her mother to Merkel Cell carcinoma in 2011.

Since completing the summits of all 15 California 14ers, Deborah and Adrian, along with their team of "usual suspects" , who you have read about in this book, have successfully climbed Mt. Rainier, completed a four-day Sierra crossing in winter, and climbed the Mexican Volcanoes among many other adventures. During those adventures, Deborah and Adrian would often discuss this book and, given their disparate backgrounds, generally disagree on correct punctuation. We apologize for any inconsistences in this book.

To contact the authors please go to http://www.climb14ers.org

During our climbs we supported STOP Cancer in our efforts to combat cancer. If you would like to donate toward the fight to find a cure for cancer please visit 'City Of Hope' at https://www.cityofhope.org

- THE END -

Made in the USA
Columbia, SC
19 April 2021